# Elven Hedgewitchery and Found Magic:

## USING ART-MAKING FOR EVOKING ELFIN MAGIC AND LIVING THE ELVEN WAY

## The Silver Elves

# DEDICATION

This book is dedicated to our beloved faerie sister **Michiko Spring** who shared her beautiful art, loving friendship, and enchantment magic with us. She was a true art therapist loving and lighting up the lives of all the many children that she served.

We also dedicate this book to our elven-ranger brother **Danyêl** who was an amazing artist and taught us to always try creating something ourselves instead of buying it ready made.

We miss them both greatly and send them elven blessings on their shining paths among the stars.

**"Ver nesidas mellun vari te!"** (Arvydase, the magical language of the Silver Elves, for "In shimmering starlight ever be")

**"ELVES CONSIDER ALL ART TO BE SPELLS OF ENCHANTMENT CAST TO TRANSFORM THE WORLD."**

—THE SILVER ELVES

# Table of Contents

# Introduction

In *Elven Hedgewitchery and Found Magic: Using Art-Making for Evoking Elfin Magic and Living the Elven Way*, we share with you many of our favorite magical elven art projects that we have enjoyed creating in the last 40+ years and give you guidance and detailed instructions for making your own and using them in your magic, along with over 100 photos to demonstrate the art processes. And even though we do demonstrate and guide you in this book on how to make the magical art that we include, it is surely not important that you do things exactly the way we have done them but that you feel inspired to do your own magical art with what material is available to you. We include our magical art processes from faerie altered clothing and making faerie houses to creating magical elf stones and ritual tools such as a book of shadows and also a scrapbook of shadows, chalices, ally dolls, wands, canes, staffs, rattles, wishing wheels and mojo bags. We further have chapters on making elfin dream pillows, fairy dust, reliquaries, elven Mbuti, paintings, illuminated circles, magic soul cards, tarot decks, pan pipes, maps and even some of our favorite elven group-art games. And our final chapter shares with you more about the Orb of Healing, which is a magical artifact that is at the center of our elven magick. Also, this is a book of elven spells and enchantment magic, with 200 elven rhyming magical spells that you may use in rituals to empower your art and magic with each magical item and creative project.

## Art and Magic

Art and magic are nearly synonymous in elven culture because elves are predisposed to art-making and it is in nearly every magical act that we do. Deep in each of us is the capacity to imagine and access internal images. In indigenous times, people drew images on walls as an expression of real life accounts as well as the illumination of their dreams and imagination. It is characteristic of the elfin to use art to both reaffirm the importance of our daily life and to reinforce our magic, charms and enchantments.

People often ask us to tell them more about how we do our magic each day and to describe our rituals. There is no better way to understand our elfin magical practices than to study our art, how we make it and how we use it (except to come spend some time with us, of course). Our art and magic are intertwined, and we are sharing with you in this book a real "how to" glimpse into our magic and enchantment spell crafting through our elven creative process of art-making.

As independent scholar Ellen Dissanayake suggests in *Homo Aestheticus: Where art comes from and why*, it is through the emotional power of both magic ritual and art-making that the two are united. We elves may say that we are doing magic, when indeed we are deeply involved in painting an elven spirit sigil on a rock for healing a loved one or busy altering a piece of our clothing to be a more elven or faerie-like costume for either ritual or everyday appearance. For the elves, every act of art is an act of magic, whether we are making an occult tool to be used in a magical ritual or decorating our home or personal attire, it is all done with magical intent and excitement.

To these elves, every altar or magic table that we design is an act of art (by the way, we elves don't call our magical working places altars, which has a certain religious connotation to it, but 'magic tables'). Even if someone buys all the items or magical tools for the magic table, the arrangement of these magical items is an art in itself. But you will find if you come into our eald (elven home), that our magic tables or altars are filled less with store bought items and more with our own magical arts and crafts, including: our handmade wands, magic rocks and rune stones that we have painted with our elven spirits and elven runes; objects we have found in nature like feathers, abandoned bird nests, shells, tree bark, twigs and leaves; handmade mojo bags and rattles; sigils we have drawn on papers; candles we have labeled with our own spells; our own handmade elven tarot cards and many of the other arts and spell crafting you will be introduced to in this book.

Our magic tables/altars are full of our own art and the reason is twofold: first, we feel that making the object is a part of our magical ritual and our own art is uniquely elven; and second, these elves have never been wealthy in any worldly way and we have never wanted to wait for the money to buy expensive magical tools like wands and crystals to perform a certain magic, thus we usually enjoy making our own. Our way has always been to make our magical items ourselves if we can not afford to buy them or find them on sale to fit our pocketbook. This does not mean that the Shining Ones have not made it possible for us to have some expensive magic table pieces (after all the magical items we buy are usually made from another person's magical hands so they, too, have their own magical power), but we have learned it is not necessary to wait for it to be possible for such-and-such to arrive to us, and we have just always preferred to make our own and love the process of spell crafting, that is crafting art with spells and vice versa.

As an example, we have a handmade prayer wheel that is now 22 years old and it still sits on one of our magic tables today. We made it originally from a condensed milk can with a wooden dowel rod we inserted as the handle with a screw going through the top of the can, attaching thus to the rod in such a way so that the can could spin, decorated the outside with magical pictures and gifted it to one of our children, who used it for magic wishing until it nearly fell apart. Still today, it is our prayer wheel of choice and contains a small paper with our family wishes inside, even though we were able to actually buy a beautiful new one when we visited Thailand a number of years ago.

Some of our magical items are tattered and old, but while their aesthetic appeal may be worn, the magic imbued in these objects has had many years to grow and deepen, and they give off a very powerful energy. Of course, this is not to say that we do not have on our magic tables throughout our eald an inordinate amount of teraphims (spirit infused figurines) that we have either bought or that have been gifted to us throughout the years, to date about 500 or more elves, faeries and otherkin. And truly, our large faerie statue that we call Violet (her eyes are violet), is perhaps the most magical of teraphim beings we have ever met. She sits upon her own large magic table along with flower leis and peacock feathers we have collected from our winged friends when they shed each Spring.

In the typical elven home, you will find a number of art projects in process at any given time. For instance, at this moment, we have in our home an acrylic painting in process on our easel, some rocks being purified to be used for painting on elven spirit sigils of protection, and a skirt in the process of being altered into an elven costume. Art and spell crafting is our way of life and an important part of our magic.

Because we elves perform spell casting throughout our art process, we have shared many elfin spells in this book that may be used with each of these acts of art and magic. Along with each craft presented, we have also included a magical image corresponding to each craft, and this may be used for meditation and entry into the faerie realms of magic.


## Hedgewitchery


What is a Hedgewitch? When we look up this word in Merriam Webster's Collegiate Dictionary, we don't find anything about a hedgewitch. However, the word hedge itself is somewhat revealing. It means a row of bushes or hedges but also a circle of protection, reminiscent of a magic circle. A hedge is, in a sense, a way of using Nature to protect ones'elf and one's loved ones.

When we look the word up online, we are told that it may have its roots in the Saxon word 'haegtessa', which is translated as 'hedge-rider' (Is the witch's broom stick from the hedge?). It further relates the word both to the idea of shamanism and the ability to commune with and communicate with spirits and the traditional idea that witches have great knowledge and use of plants and herbs. The Urban Dictionary adds an additional meaning of a hedgewitch being attuned with Higher Consciousness, although we'd say being attuned to Higher Consciousness through attunement to and communion with Nature.

There is another way to look at it. In Lev Grossman's trilogy of *The Magicians* and the SyFy channel series based upon it, there are wizards and witches that are formally trained in schools such as Brakebills and there are outsiders, street magicians, who have no formal training but who are sharing their knowledge and training thems'elves with each other. These street magicians or less formally trained magic wielders would be hedgewitches from an elven point of view.

In *Icelandic Magic: Practical Secrets of the Northern Grimoires* by Stephen E. Flowers Ph.D., he speaks of Icelandic Magic being a syncretized blending of Norse traditions, Western Ceremonial Magic and the Latin texts of the ancients. But there are other traditions, less formal traditions that existed in that same culture at the same time (as is the case in most other cultures as well). These are the folk traditions of magic, or what these days is often referred to as Hoodoo as evidenced by *Trolldom: Spells and Methods of the Norse Folk Magic Tradition* by Johannes Björn Gårdbäck and edited by our long-time friend Catherine Yronwode who runs the Lucky Mojo Curio Company. It is also referred to as rootwork, as well as various other names.

As Flowers points out in his book, even during the height of the witch hunts of the middle ages, those who practiced what we might call educated magic or some might say high magic, those who came from wealth, were seldom effected by or accused of witchcraft. And if they were, then a few bribes here and there usually did the trick for getting them off (life hasn't changed much). But for the poor witch, the hedgewitch, the commoner, if you were accused you were tortured until you confessed and once you confessed you were killed. Notice the difference between those who were persecuted for witchcraft in Elizabethan times and her own court wizard and astrologer, Dr. John Dee, who was protected due to his connection to the crown. It pays to have important friends. Also, note that as Flowers points out in his book, many of those who practiced what we might call High Magic, or rich magic, we might say, or school educated magic, if you will, were often priests or religious officials.

In certain ways, this prejudice against lay-workers or laity of magic, as we like to call them, or hedgewitches, was similar to the current practice that only certified doctors can practice medicine, and everyone else has to put a disclaimer that their remedies may or may not work, even though doctors are not always able to cure people either. Homeopaths and those who offer herbal remedies are simply not given the same respect, for the most part, that those who have been to medical school have and there is some justice to this, but still, this is an ancient prejudice that still carries on today and has some part in the witch trials of yesteryear.

Alternative medicine, which in a sense is to say hedgewitchery, can be a bit dangerous for the practitioner, not as much as it once was but still it takes a bit of daring. Most of what doctors do, even if it doesn't work, is seen as scientific, whereas what hedgewitches do, what Hoodoo practitioners do, even if it does work, is seen as superstitious.

In Elven tradition, there is not quite the strict line between formally educated magic and hedgewitchery, or s'elf educated or street magic. Perhaps this is true in part because most magic wielders of these days have to be at least a bit and usually quite a bit s'elf educated, gaining our understanding though practice and sharing our knowledge with each other. However, these elves were definitely raised by hedgewitches, even though they would not have called thems'elves that or thought of thems'elves in that way, they simply passed on the folk traditions of magic that their ancestors had passed down to them. Simple magics but ancient traditions none-the-less.

Yet, it is true we were also educated by the Elf Queen's Daughters, who were quite adept enchanters, in the use of the I Ching, drawing up and interpreting an astrology chart, necromancy and many other magic arts and sciences and whether one wishes to consider this a sort of school of magic or hedgewitchery, we leave to the individual.

## Found and Free Magic

Often in books about magic, people talk of making wands by going to a tree, finding an appropriate branch, thanking the tree for its donation, sometimes asking it for permission first and intuiting the answer and so on and then cutting off the branch. In old stories of witchcraft, spells are often put together using an herbal concoction, so to speak, with the eye of newt (very popular apparently) and tail of salamander and so forth. We elves prefer found magic. We don't go to the forest or nearby woods and cut a branch from a tree, rather we find a branch that has fallen or that we have otherwise come across and use as the basic part of our wands accepting it as a sort of gift from the Earth and the Universe, which is to say from the Divine Magic.

This, to us, is part of our elven hedgewitchery. The gifts of Nature are abundant and most of the magical items we create are gifts of Nature, or sometimes gifts from other folk, or most often a combination thereof. It is sometimes said that nothing in life is free, and yet these elves have all sorts of things that we have come by freely, without theft, mind you, that we use in our magical creations. Buttons come to us, pieces of jewelry (some of these broken but still usable for our art), clothes, cloth, ribbon, lace, embroidery thread and sewing thread, wire, string, cord, and all sorts of things as you will discover as you explore this magical tome of elven art — the elven art, really, of making magic.

For over forty years, we have been making elf stones or spirit rocks, as we sometimes call them, and sending them around the world. Sometimes, we give them to friends who are going to distant places and ask them to leave it in the wild somewhere, among the trees or bushes or by a stream. In the last decade, we're been given the privilege of adventuring overseas ours'elves, carrying these rocks with us and placing them in woodlands and other magical spots around the globe. But we have, in the past, also placed them in our work places before we retired and other places where we wished to use our magic to influence the ambience of the place and make it favorable for us and others working there.

We use rocks of a certain size, fairly flat on two sides is best, and we create a symbol or utilize one of our elf runes (see our book *The Book of Elven Runes*) or a spirit sigil from our book of spirits (*An Elfin Book of Spirits* that has 360 spirits with their sigils in it) and paint the symbol on one side of the stone and then paint the essential meaning of the symbol upon the other, such as Elf Magic, or Faerie Awakening. In time we learned to put sealant over the painted sigil so it would last and endure, especially since these rocks are often placed outdoors in Nature and subject to the dictates of the weather. Although, we often hope that someone will eventually find them and receive them as a gift of magic and a blessing into their life (see more on our magical elf stones in Chapter 15).

However, we have certain rules concerning the collection of these elf stones. Not only do we need a certain size and shape but they need to come to us freely. By that we mean, we don't take rocks from someone's yard where they have piled up or spread out dozens, sometimes hundreds, of these type of stones for decorative purposes. Even though most, or all, of them are the right size and shape, we don't take from someone else's art, so to speak. For us, the rock we get needs to be on its own or with just one other and clearly somewhat out of place, as most of us who are elves and elfae are in this world anyway. They stand out in that way. They call to us and it is clear that they don't belong to anyone in particular nor have been placed there to beautify a person's home or garden. They are found magic and freely given in a sense, although the giver in this case is Nature, circumstance and the Divine Magic itself.

This is not to say that we never invest anything in our creations. Sometimes we may have to buy glue, or invest in the sealant previously mentioned or some other thing to help put the magical object together, but at least 90% or greater of the objects we use in our art are things we have found, been gifted, or come by for free—things that we got for free often abandoned on a table at the end of the day at a swap meet where we had a shop and did tarot readings for $1 for over 15 years, usually left by someone who asked too much for it and wound up just leaving it; or that we found on a table in the building where we live where residents put things they no longer wanted; or things that have been re-gifted to us; or even on occasions that we found on the side of the road or sidewalk awaiting the disposal truck. Some things we have saved for years, even decades, awaiting the right creation to be a part of. For we will find the primary piece, a shaft of wood for a wand, or a bit of clothing to be transformed into an elven raiment or some other thing, and this piece will be the heart of the magical artwork. And then we will search through all the things we have saved for years, looking until we find the right combination of objects to create a magical tool that fulfills our imaginal vision and satisfies us soulfully.

As it happens, we don't do a lot of eye of newt type of magic, but if we did we wouldn't go around killing creatures to use their body parts in our spells. How do you preserve a newt's eye anyway? Eyes disintegrate quickly after death. Do you kill a newt just to pluck out its eye? That just seems wrong and somewhat crazy to these elves. However, we have found in Nature and collected bird feathers of various sorts — turkey feathers, quail feathers, parrot feathers, pheasant feathers, house sparrow feathers, peacock feathers — as well as the dried up bodies of bumblebees, moths, geckos, the skin of our iguana named Binkie that would shed her snake-like skin periodically, a claw that was shed by our dog Elfie, and various other creatures and their gifts and if we needed such things as part of our spells, we would use these objects that had been freely given. Found magic! Elven hedgewitchery!

It is a bit of a challenge really. Finding the right things, collecting the right things, awaiting the right combination and then putting them all together. But that, too, is part of the magic.

## Spells, Enchantments and Incantations

This is a book of magic — a very practical magic that involves the creation of one's magical tools, which include wands, staffs, rattles, crowns, hoods, robes and many other instruments of magic and, in this case in particular, of elven magic and enchantment. So it is only natural that we include spells (of which there are 200) in this book for all magical items that you can use in charging your instruments and tools. Of course, you can always make up your own or alter them as needed.

However, the spell you use may vary with the purpose of the tool you are making. For instance, wands might be made for a variety of specific purposes. It is also possible that a wand would be an all-purpose or general purpose wand, like a doctor who is a general practitioner rather than a specialist, but it is also possible to have a wand for a specific purpose. Usually other tools, such as a ring of power have a particular ability associated with them. The One Ring of Tolkien's lore, for instance, gave the wearer the power of invisibility, although curiously, it did the opposite for Sauron and seemed to give him substance. Perhaps it related to the plane the individual wearing it was on. If the person was a regular material being, it would make them invisible, which is to say, less material, but if the person was a more etheric being, such as Sauron, it gave him power and form in the material world. Most magical items are of this nature, seven league boots, invisibility cloaks and so on, each offering a specific power. So we offer you a variety of spells that reflect the usual uses of the magical item in question.

In casting spells, you can surely wait until you are done and then cast a spell or enchantment upon the item. But you may wish to chant a spell at the beginning of construction and now and again while you are creating the tool. This is a more powerful way of spell casting, but there may be times when you may actually need to concentrate on making the item in question and letting the spell float in the air around it, so to speak. Do what feels best to you and trust your instincts and intuition in this regard.

You will notice that most of the spells are rhyming or chanting spells and might be called mantras, which is not to say that all mantras are rhymed, although most elven mantras/spells are. This is not only because we Silver Elves love making up little rhymes but also because traditionally spells are often rhymed. Rhymed enchantments are easy to remember and create a certain vibration and radiance in their rhyme, which is a certain magic all in itself and has a bit of a hypnotic or trance effect to it as well. So when doing the incantation, make it vibrant, let it hum or sing in your mind or as you resonant it out loud. Remember, the Universe is made of energy, vibrating at various frequencies. In vibrating your spell, you are attuning to Nature and the Universe. The frequency will depend upon your own voice that will make it perfectly suited to you, your nature and your specific enchantment.

But don't forget intention. The spell is just the conduit for your intent. Your imagination is of vital importance in this, so visualize, which is to say imagine the energy you desire weaving itself into the magical item and filling it with that energy. As well as, imagine the item preforming the magical power you are instilling into it. Now, you are doing magic and the magic will radiate from the items you have created ever after. Or, as it is said at the end of every good Fairy Tale, happily ever after.

However, we might add that every spell we do, every item/art we enchant, bears with it certain aspects. The item can never be used to harm the innocent. If it is found, the magic, its powers and its blessings goes to the finder, with the previously mentioned proviso. If it is destroyed, either accidentally or intentionally, or stolen, the magic returns to us and the Universe. You might call this a sort of magical insurance policy.

**All 200 spells in this book are written in both English and Arvyndase, the magical language of the Silver Elves, with an Arvyndase pronounciation guide for saying each spell.**

**"The Elves say: Be careful what you witch for."**

"Elves are enchanters,
We enchant every day,
We enchant in the morning,
We enchant on our way,
We enchant as the stars give light to the night,
'Neath the moon that is glowing softly or bright,
We enchant as we lay to slip off to sleep,
We enchant in our dreams for the magic to keep,
All our beloved safe and fulfilled,
As we've enchanted, and just as we've willed."

—The Silver Elves

# Chapter 1 . . . . Altering Clothes into Faerie Attire

Designing and altering clothing is a natural skill for elves. Some of us have been experimenting with altering our clothing to look more elven magical since we were very small children. Silver Flame remembers that when she was a child she disappointed her parents when she cut one blouse of her new back-to-school clothing up a bit, to alter the sleeves to look more faerie-like. Zardoa used to take his old uniforms from military school and alter them into costumes. But this elven tendency to redesign our clothing can, with a few sewing skills, become a lucrative profession, as faerie style clothing has become quite popular in the modern age. Each day we go out, we nearly always see at least one flowing jagged-cut faerie skirt on a tourist walking down the streets of Waikiki where we live. We have noticed that they are particularly popular among Japanese tourists as well as the tourists from the US mainland. But popular or not, elves and otherkin have been wearing them for decades and this is just one example of how we love to alter our clothing to fit our magically enchanting appearance.

**The Magical Image:** *Three faery sisters weave glittered threads into their flowing gowns and dance away into the woodland dale.*

## Hoods

One of the simplest ways to turn a common coat, cloak, robe, dress, sweater, or shirt into an enchanting elven look is to add a hood. So that is why we are beginning this section on clothes altering with directions and suggestions for hood-making. After all, elves are the original hoody people. Surely Robin Hood, or Robin in the Hood, was an elfin being, or if not, raised by the elves, for after all he had his merry (read elven) men about him, and we expect merry women as well.

We first began making hoods when Zardoa decided he wanted to wear one for sleeping, to keep his head warm. He also finds it convenient for helping him to sleep during long airline journeys, although he is not very good at sleeping on planes, overall. We found hoods so easy to make that we have since made many, with velvet or satin being our favorite fabrics to use, although satin can be slippery. Usually, we find bits of velvet, and you can frequently buy velvet inexpensively or reasonably priced among the scraps or leftover section of material stores. We have also used old velvet skirts or shirts for this, but you can also find old tablecloths with nice patterns on them that you can use. Really, it's quite easy to find material that will work for a hood and it doesn't actually require that much material in the first place.

Hoods can be worn instead of a hat for any costume or attached to a garment like a coat to become an elven robe. We often like to make hoods for specific magical events and meditations or special full moon spell casting, adorning them with a variety of appropriate gems for the magic they will bring to the occasion. For sleeping, of course, unadorned is usually best, but for costuming you may consider a variety of jewelry pins or other adornments that will make your hood memorable, more elven and very special.

**The Magical Image:** *The elven magician wears hir hood to silently slip through the woods as sHe returns to hir eald.*

## Materials Needed:

- About 1 square yard of material (or more if you would like to make a lining)
- Measuring tape
- Scissors
- Pattern making paper
- Thread to match hood material, needles and straight pins
- Ornaments like tassels, ribbons and jewelry
- Frog clasps

## Directions:

Perhaps the easiest way to make a hood is to find one that fits you on a jacket and trace it, also leaving room for a seam. If you do not have a hood to copy, then you will first need to measure your neckline. The bottom edge of the hood needs to measure ½ of the neckline of the garment you are sewing it on  (plus room for the seam, about ⅝ inches) or ½ of your own neckline if you are making it as a stand alone hood. To the right above, you can see the basic shape of a hood pattern. We use whatever we have on hand as pattern making paper, including: regular artist tracing paper, brown craft paper or butcher paper.

To make your pattern, you have already measured the neckline and cut the bottom edge of the pattern from the directions above. Next, to complete the pattern, you need to measure from your shoulder to the top of your head and the hood pattern should measure the same from the bottom to the top of the hood. Now measure from the back of your head (center) to the front side of your head (to your temples), adding at least 1 inch, and this gives you the width of the pattern.

Now turn the hood material inside out and fold the cloth in half. Place your pattern on the material, then cut all the way around. You can place the pattern on the fold of the material (this will leave one less side to sew together later), but we do not usually do this because you can use less material if you position your pattern on the material sideways.

Next sew along the back curve from the bottom to the top front. Now turn the hood right side out. This leaves the front open where your face will be facing and the bottom open to sew onto your coat or other garment. Now fold under the seam on the face and tack it under. The last step is to turn the seam under on the bottom side and sew the hood onto the coat on that bottom seam. You may need to remove the collar to the coat and have an open seam to attach it to (see directions for altering a coat into a robe a bit further in this chapter).

Now don't forget to adorn your hoods that you use for costumes, elven style! We like to sew beautiful buttons, ribbons, or pieces of broken jewelry on the middle front of the hood. Or, we might find a colorful feather and sew it on the side.

We also make a lot of stand-alone hoods. They can be used with any costume and are simple to make. To the right is an example of a pattern for a stand-alone hood; however, it looks narrower in the photo than it is in reality. You can see the basic hood shape is a little different from the hood pattern for adding to a coat as it has a small extension coming out of the neck. Also note the outline of a ⅝ inch seam all the way around.

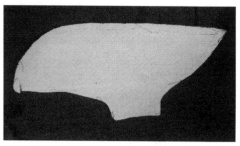

You can make a stand-alone hood out of old clothing; we have made them out of sleeves of dresses and shirts and once Zardoa even made a magnificent hood out of a woman's skirt! So be on the lookout for beautiful material, even if it is a garment you would not wear, you well might be able to do a bit of faerie altering and have a beautiful hood for all magical occasions. Here are a few photos of some of our hood creations:

**(Left) Simple stand-alone hood; (Right) Zardoa wearing a light blue velvet hood with center jewel.**

(Left) Zardoa in elf hood hat made from a shirtsleeve of beautiful dark blue velvet.
(Right) Zardoa in Santa Elf hood. Just add some fur (faux) around the brim to a basic hood
and leave the hood back end point open, adorned with fur about ten inches from the end.

One of our favorite hoods to make is an Elven Hood Wrap and it uses a square yard piece of cloth. We have even sewn together a couple of random pieces of cloth into a square yard to use for this, so just let your creativity flow. 1.) First turn the material inside out and then fold it over one time and sew up all the way around except for a small place on one side where you can reach in and pull it out (once sewn all the way around) so it is right side showing. 2.) Fold under and sew up the one little opening that you used to turn it to the right side. 3.) Then put it evenly over your head and find a place that is comfortable under your chin to sew it from there to the bottom, leaving the back open, draping down the back. 4.) Sew on a tassel on each side at the middle of the neck. Now you can just tie the tassels in the back.

(Left) You can see where the Elven Hood Wrap is sewn up under Zardoa's chin to the bottom of the front; Right) Zardoa models a wrapping hood with tassels on the sides that are tied in the back.

An even simpler method of making a wrap hood is our Elven Triangle Hood Wrap: 1. Start with a big square (square yard). Then we simply fold it into a triangle and sew up the two sides (We suggest that you turn it inside out and leave a space to pull it through like you did in making the wrap hood on the previous page). We add frogs to the two top point ends and wrap it around fastening it with the frogs. The third point has a beautiful tassel attached.

**(Left) Zardoa models a red velvet Elven Triangle Hood Wrap with a jewel attached to the front. (Right) Frogs on two sides clasp the hood in the back.**

Another hood that we created, we designed to go around our elf pointy ears (did we say that we love wearing elf ears?). Because, what is the point of wearing a hood (unless it is really cold) if you can't show off your elven ears? In this case, we simply took the cloth for the hood, put it over our head and  used chalk to outline where the ears would be, leaving a little extra for sewing it together, for our hoods most often have a lining usually of the same cloth, and cut out the area for the ears to show. Also, it may be  that you will need to bring two sides together (if you don't have a single piece large enough), and sew them together along the top and down the back. The length of the material in front of the ears is up to you, but you may wish to consider making it long enough to tie together or have frogs or other connectors on them.

The same is true of the back of the hood behind your ears. You surely wish it to come down to your neck, but you may wish it to be longer than that. That is a stylistic and decorative decision. Will it be pointed, or flat across at the end, or what? Will you hang a tassel on it? It's up to you. Also, if you wish to have the back top of the hood pointed, leave extra material for it. In our case, we not only had that part pointed out from the back of the head, but folded it up and over upon itself so it pointed up and forward, a bit like a Phrygian Cap but pointing toward the front. To achieve this we not only folded and sewed the fold forward but also stuffed it with a bit of batting so it would stay upward.

## Elven Spell Casting

What exactly do you wish your elf hood for? Does it have a purpose? If it is for sleeping that would be one spell. If it is a hood for enchanting, by which in this case we mean attracting attention and contributing to the aura of an elven costume, that would be a different spell. Or it could be for camouflage or hiding, which is to say not being noticed but rather escaping notice and attention, as a ranger might desire for their hood. And that would be another spell entirely. We give you a sampling of possibilities. If you have some other purpose, you can always make up your own spell.

**Also, as we have previously noted, you will notice that the spells will be in English and then have our Arvyndase translation after, with the pronunciation following that.** There is just something magical and enchanting about reciting one's spells in Arvyndase (see our books *Arvyndase (Silverspeech): A Short Course in the Magical Language of the Silver Elves* and *The Complete Dictionary of Arvyndase: The Elven Language of the Silver Elves*).

SLEEPING SPELL:
**"Blissful sleep comes easily
Deeply healing, sets me free."**

(Arvyndase)
**"Elsyndas anu kosolu hamla
Dorala hyrndas, påndlu el alo."**

(Pronunciation)
Eel - sin - dace a - new co - so - lou haim - lah
Door - ray - lah herne - dace, pond - lou eel a – low.

ENCHANTMENT SPELL:
**"Wonder in the eyes of all
This hood my elfin kin doth call."**

(Arvyndase)
**"Tyltål ver tae arli u wyl
Wyr verd el'na êldat eldi båver koar."**

(Pronunciation)

Till - tahl veer tay air - lie you will

Were veerd eel'nah l - date eel - dye bah - veer co – air.

**DISGUISE SPELL:**
**"Here I am but none do see**
**I come and go, like breeze through tree."**

(Arvyndase)
**"Jän El da kana konar ba ten**
**El koso nar tas, sylar soran joul alda."**

(Pronunciation)

Jan eel dah kay - nah co - nair bah teen

Eel co - so nair tace, sill - lair so - rain joe - yule ale – dah.

**STEALTH SPELL** (similar to "Disguise spell" but for a slightly different purpose):
**"Unseen on through the world I go**
**Not sound, nor sense, nor sight doth show."**

(Arvyndase)
**"Murtenïn ton joul tae telth El tas**
**Kon deth, konsa fen, konsa terad båver teke."**

(Pronunciation)

Muir - teen - in tone joe - yule tay teal-th Eel tace

Cone deeth, cone - sah feen, cone - sah tea - raid bah - veer tea – key.

## Hooded Coats

One of our favorite articles of clothing we love to faery alter is a coat. Zardoa loves coats and cloaks and has about a dozen. We offer the following example of one of our creations with faery altering a coat for and by Zardoa. We realize that it is unlikely that you will ever find the exact same coat and so will not be doing the exact same altering. The idea is not to create an identical coat but to inspire you in creating one that is unique/elven to you. But we think this will give you an idea of how the process goes.

Mostly, we suggest that you save all scraps of material and buttons that you find beautiful and when you find a garment that is worthy of altering in order to make it a bit more magical and elven/faerie, that you feel free to cut, sew and practice altering. Once we were told by a great artist that the key to learning to paint is to not be afraid to get paint on yours'elf, and to just keep on putting more and more paint on the canvas until you arrive at something that feels good to you. Altering clothing is similar in that you need to be brave and daring enough to cut and sew on a garment, and to keep on practicing until you learn what works for you. The following is one of our coat altering experiences, although you may wish to begin with a smaller garment like a shirt or sweater.

One November, we were on our way to Thailand and had packed clothes for hot weather. But we were delayed overnight unexpectedly in Narita, Japan, where it was quite cold. We took the train to the old part of town to visit the Narita Town temple and on our way found a small used clothing store where we both bought coats from a sweet Japanese lady who was in the process of opening her shop. Unfortunately, there were few coats to pick from, so Zardoa ended up with a coat that was quite large for him and that was made to fit a person (a woman, we think) much shorter than Zardoa and much wider.

A couple of years later when we were faerie altering some clothes, we turned this coat into one of our favorite costume coats/cloaks. Now with his new cloak and magical staff (see our section on making staffs), Zardoa was ready for the Halloween Street Ball in Waikiki 2016 (see photo to the left of Zardoa and Silver Flame on their way to the Ball). By the way, Halloween is jam-packed in Waikiki. You can barely walk up and down the street and the crowds are so large that you move about a foot every five seconds, with thousands of people in costumes and myriads of international and US tourists gawking and taking photos. In the past few years, Japanese tourists have gotten more and more into dressing up themselves to join in the fun (Halloween is celebrated in Japan although not an official holiday and only since the year 2000), so the Waikiki Halloween Street Ball is full of excited Japanese tourists).

So now let's retrace the steps we used in making this most magical elven hooded coat.

**The Magical Image:** *The wizard faerie alters an old coat he finds into a magical cloak and wears it to a masquerade party.*

## Materials Needed:

You will need a coat or cloak that you plan to alter, an iron, scraps of leather large enough to cut two panels about 3 by 2 ft. each, another piece that is approximately 2 by 1 ft., and another that is large enough to cut two cuffs (about 1 ft. by 1 ft. each). Also, you need marking chalk, 12 matching medium-large size buttons, needle and thread to match the coat.

**<u>Directions:</u>**

Here are the coat altering steps Zardoa used on his coat, with some pictures:

1.  Since it was too wide for Zardoa, we took it up in the back by creating a V toward the shoulders—becoming a straight line down the back (see photo below).

2.  To lengthen the coat, we added to each side of the bottom of the coat two pieces of leather that we had found for free years before on a table at our local flee market.

3.  Then we added a hood that we made out of the same leather. See the previous section on how to make a hood.

4.  Next, we took what was left of the leather and extended the cuffs so they were long enough to turn up and be a decorative French style cuff (like a pirate coat sleeve).

5.  There were only two buttons on the front and Zardoa wanted more. He wanted the coat to be able to be open with buttons on each side like a military coat. So we added four more buttons on the one side to make 6 and then 6 buttons on the opposite side too. This also meant we needed to create more buttonholes (using the existing two button holes as a template size to create more holes). So we cut the holes on one side and then using embroidery thread, we sewed them. We used blue thread to add color and match the bluish purple leather that we had already added on the coat. Using the 6 holes that were now on the one side to measure where the buttonholes on the other side would go, we traced them (using sewing chalk) and cut those holes too, then sewed them up.

6.  Now that the buttonholes were all made, we folded back the front lapel on each side of the coat to mark where the buttons should go. Then we sewed on all the buttons (6 on each side)

7.  Next, we created 3 buttonholes on each cuff and sewed on buttons to match.

8.  And last, we added one piece to the right shoulder to make a cape like flap. We used a section of black faux fur that we had also found for free at a yard sale and cut it around its edges to give a more natural shape to it—this and the leather we had on hand, saved in our scraps container. The last step was to add a beautiful pin onto the fur flap, just for decoration.

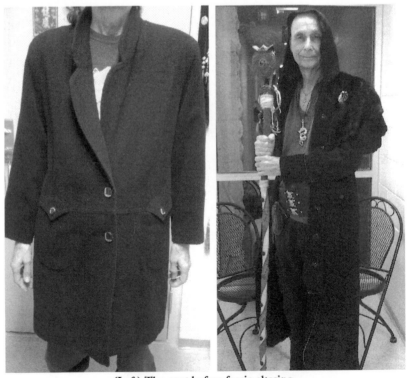

**(Left) The coat before faerie altering,**
**(Right) In stunning faerie altered coat, Zardoa is now ready for the ball in elven style!**

## Elven Spell Casting

**INVISIBILITY SPELL:**
"I am here and yet unseen
Until the time that I do deem."

(Arvyndase)
"El da jän nar nov murtenïn
Murted tae mern dij El bah ot."

(Pronunciation)
Eel dah jan nair know-v muir - teen - in
Muir - teed tay mere-n dye-j Eel bah oat.

**ENCHANTMENT SPELL:**
"Wondrous and beautiful, elegant and fair
Everyone who sees me must stop and pause and stare."

(Arvyndase)
"Tyltålsey nar eloåfel, elådan nar faer
Lotymata jae tenlu el sarb vird nar bers nar norv."

(Pronunciation)
Till - tahl - say nair e - low - ah - feel, e - lah - dane nair fay - ear
Low - tim - a - tah jay teen - lou eel sayr-b vier-d nair beers nair nor-v.

**PROTECTION SPELL:**
"Shielded am I from all harm
By this coat's protective charm."

(Arvyndase)
"Yandïn da El an wyl gras
La wyr safyr'na kafåko elfat."

(Pronunciation)
Yeah-nd - in da Eel ane will grace
Lah were say - fer'nah kay - fah - co eel – fate.

**EVOCATION SPELL:**
(if you use the coat as one might use a robe for ritual or ceremonial magick workings):
**"Great the powers that I wield**
**To my will the world doth yield."**

(Arvyndase)
**"Ralt tae eldro dij El yot**
**Va el'na yon tae telth båver ped."**

(Pronunciation)
Rail-t tay eel - drow [like row] dye-j eel yote
Vah  eel'na yone tay tealth bah - veer peed.

## Elven Leaf Shoes

We like to experiment altering to make everything elven, including our shoes. A simple way to do this is to take an old pair of sandals and glue some artificial leaves or flowers (of course you could use live cut ones but it would not last long) on the shoes.

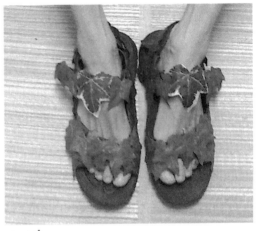

Here is an example of a pair of old sandals that we have glued artificial ivy leaves all over in rows to cover the shoe (see photo on the right). We used Sobo craft and fabric glue. Just use your imagination and what you have handy: feathers, shells, flowers, leaves, or twigs. And for extra fun, alter an old purse to match.

As it is, we discovered that we seldom include our feet in out photos —most photos of us being taken from the waist upward. Therefore, Zardoa uses these sandals mostly when we go swimming in what a Hawaiian friend of ours once referred to as the "Hawaiian swimming pool," by which he meant the Pacific Ocean. Since we live just a couple of streets from Waikiki Beach, it is easy to put on our swimming suits, don our elven sandals, and stroll over for a swim.

## Elven Spell Casting

**SPEED SPELL:** (most enchanted boots, shoes or sandals have to do with the power of speed or of covering large distances quickly, such as the legendary Seven League Boots that can take one seven leagues in a single step)

"Quick I move and swift arrive
Soon to be wherever I strive."

(Arvyndase)
"Zif El ral nar vys komal
Qun va te nasvari El tru."

(Pronunciation)
Zie-f Eel rail nair viss co - male
Que-n vah tea nace - vair - rye Eel true.

**ENDURANCE SPELL:** (you could do an endurance spell to make your shoes last, but this one is intended to enable you to walk as long as needed in the enchanted footwear without ever tiring)
"I do walk and never tire
Ascending the heights to which I aspire."

(Arvyndase)
"El bah talf nar konzar sta
Rystardas tae altarli va tild El watan."

(Pronunciation)
Eel bah tale-f nair cone - zair stah
Riss - tair - dace tay ale - tair - lie vah tile-d Eel way – tane.

**STYLE SPELL:** (Men, we are told, say that you can judge a person by the shoes they wear. Women surely seem to believe this to be so. We elves, on the other hand, find this to be a rather superficial point of view. None-the-less, faerie or elfin shoes can be quite wonderous to behold and can add to any elfin costume)
"Behold their wonder and their grace
That makes their mark with every pace."

(Arvyndase)
"Edonfåïn tam'na tyltål nar tam'na darsh
Dij kordlu tam'na murd ena lotym ob."

(Pronunciation)
E - doan - fah - in tame'nah till - tahl nair tame'nah dare-sh
Dye-j cord - lou tame'nah muir-d e - nah low - tim ohb

**STEALTH SPELL:**
**"Soft my footfall, never heard**
**Slip through the world undisturbed."**

(Arvyndase)
**"Deso el'na bondnor, konzar lysïn**
**Sof joul tae telth murbothïn."**

(Pronunciation)
Dee - so eel'nah boned - nor, cone - zair liss - in
So-f joe - yule tay teal-th muir - both – in.

## Faerie-Dyeing

Most cloth dyes are carcinogenetic, so we do not advise that you do this art process often, if at all. But we will include it because we (prior to knowing it was so dangerous) had a lot of fun every week faerie-dyeing clothing for seven years and selling them at the local flea market. If you do it, please wear a good mask, long rubber gloves, and a scarf around your hair. Also use liquid rather than powder dyes for less chance of it being airborne and breathing it. And, work outside in the fresh air, if at all possible.

There are some alternative clothing dyes that are natural and we urge you to experiment with these plant dyes. Even if the colors are not as bright and a bit muted, they will give a beautiful blend. We once tried blueberries and also red onionskins and found that they did give a nice tint to the cloth. Turmeric makes a nice yellow. We found that Peach leaves turn cloth a yellowish green. You may be able to find others that are richer in color. With natural dyes, it is important to soak your garments in one part vinegar to four parts water (remember to use vinegar for plant dyes and salt for berry dyes). To make a natural dye, place the berries or plant in a pan of water on the stove and bring it to a boil and simmer for a half hour. For the unnatural dyes, you do not need to go through this preparation, but you will need to be sure to take precautions not to have the dye spread out into your natural environment (we will talk about how to do that in the directions).

The process of faerie-dyeing is much like tie-dyeing, except there is no tying involved, just some minor folding. Of course, if you would like to add binding spells to your art, then tying is fine to do too and we often have done this with both excellent artistic and magical effects as a result.

**The Magical Image:** *A tribe of elves laugh and sing as they dip and dye their clothing in colors of sea blue and deep purple.*

## Materials to Collect:

To faerie-dye, you need to first collect all the white or light colored cotton, lace trimmed, silk, or other natural cloth clothing that you would like to transform (some nylons and polyesters do also work but they don't take dye well). Don't worry if there is a light stain on it because you will be covering that up (which sometimes is how we get the clothes inexpensively or for free). In the photo to the right, Silver Flame is wearing some of her faerie-dyed clothing at her booth where she sold her creations. If you could see this photo in color, you would notice that her entire outfit is in a beautiful blend of light turquoise and lavender. Her long lace scarf and lacy over blouse took the dye well, as lace generally does. Hanging behind her is a nylon petticoat for sale that is also one of her creations in the same beautiful blended colors. She sold locally hundreds of her faerie-dyes over the seven-year period that she made them and if you  walked down the street of Sebastopol, California, during the 90s, you would most likely see at least one person walking about wearing one of her creations. But when people would refer to her as a tie-dye artist, she would laugh because to her faerie-dyeing was just doing what came natural, having fun playing with colors, and something anyone could do if they wished.

We like to collect scarves, wedding gowns, slips and other lingerie, belts, long white gloves, lace gloves or anything lace, hats, and any old dresses, blouses, pants and skirts we would like to faerie beautify. Perhaps, most fun of all is to faerie-dye a pair of translucent or sheer cloth fairy wings and ribbons that go with them. Curtains also work quite well and look beautiful adorning a window. You would be surprised what will faerie-dye into something magically stunning.

You will need two buckets. These buckets will get dyed, so be sure they do not need to be used for cleaning in the future. Art stores carry clothing dye. Using two different colors of dye (we like purple and turquoise and in our experience it is pretty much everyone else's favorite color combination, as well), add the clothing dye to the proper amount of water in each bucket, according to the directions on the bottle. You can use a third color (and then you will of course need a third bucket, but we rarely found three necessary, although occasionally we found a bit of fuchsia was a nice addition). You may also add one cup of vinegar per gallon of water/dye to help set the color. Of course, for elf costume dying, various shades of green may be called for and for brownies, various browns and russet tones, and sometimes a bit of brownish yellow. Faeries, of course, can go wildly rainbow in their tastes. But it is all up to you. Don't trust what lore and legend and modern stories have told you about yours'elf and your tastes, so much as trusting your own sense of fashion and your natural inclinations and your personal artistic inspiration.

## Directions:

It is best to work outside in your yard (less messy) and since the water you will be using is cold, you can use your outside hose to fill the buckets. We always put heavy plastic down under the buckets and area where we worked to catch any run off of dye so it would not get into the grass and hurt the plant and animal life. Once you have added and mixed the colors into the water, you are ready to begin the dying process.

Take a piece of clothing that you have collected, fold it over a few times (even twist it a little), and then dip it into one bucket of color. We usually start with the lightest color, but it really does not matter. Leave it in the first color only about 15 seconds. Now pull it out, and with it still folded, dip it in the second color for 15 seconds. Pull it out and open it up. If you need a little more color on it, then dip again. You have to use your intuition and artistic eye! So loosen up your arms and hands and dip away into the beautiful colors. When you faerie-dye, you are really over-dying the cloth, not tie-dying (although you may use rubber-bands and do so if you wish). Here you have to use your own creativity and just dip and mix the colors, experimenting with effects.

Now throw the dyed garment into a strong garage bag. And then fold and dip your next piece. You can throw all the dyed pieces of the same colors in the same sack. After you have finished all your pieces, you may have a full bag of faerie-dyed clothing. Let the pieces remain in the bag about an hour to set the colors, then take each piece out and give them a rinse with the hose. It is best environmentally if you can take the effort to rinse each piece in a small tub and pour the water off in a bucket to be put down a drain (rather than just using a hose in your yard). Next hang the clothing out to dry on a clothesline. However, the clothesline will be dyed too so do not expect to use it for your other clothing. In fact, for years Silver Flame hung her freshly faerie dyed clothes on our regular rope clothesline and all of Zardoa's clothes wound up getting dye spots on them, so he started wearing black clothing all the time and went through a sort of serendipitous Goth period. On the other hand, Zardoa wore all black for most of his undergraduate career and was essentially Goth, long before Goth existed as a movement. Probably, the dark elfin side of his heritage. Once they are dry, be sure and bring them out of the sun so they do not fade. You can also use a clothes dyer if you do not have a place for a clothesline, but it may get some dye in the dryer, so you will have to clean it thoroughly before using it for anything other than black clothes.

## Elven Spell Casting

**CAMOUFLAGE SPELL:** (We'd like to say that we elves invented camouflage but the truth is we learned it from the insects, fish and other creatures that mimic their surroundings. But we expect that Men might have picked up the trick from us.)
**"You look direct but do not see**

Mistaken for the brush and tree."

(Arvyndase)
**"Le shi stran kana ba kon ten**
**Zerrudta fro tae hoft nar alda."**

(Pronunciation)
Lee shy strain kay - nah bah cone teen
Zeer - rude - tah fro tay hoof-t nair ale – dah.

**FAERIE ENCHANTMENT SPELL:** (Let's face it, faeries usually like to be noticed. Especially, in the modern world, yet they have a way of seeming rather normal, or perhaps just a bit off center when doing so.)
**"You want to stare, oh, yes, you do**
**I'm fabulous, and this is true."**

(Arvyndase)
**"Le mem va norv, tra, ale, le ba**
**El'da osagra, nar wyr da lod."**
(Pronunciation)
"Lee meem vah nor-v, trah, a - lee, lee bah
Eel'dah oh - say - grah, nair were dah load."

**TRANSFORMATION SPELL:** (Faerie dyeing is about transformation in its essence. So use this garment to help you transform. It is a useful spell particularly for shapeshifters.)
**"Before your very eyes I change**
**Everything I rearrange."**

(Arvyndase)
**"Lokan le'na lefa arli El dyls**
**Lotymjart El lopatun."**

(Pronunciation)
"Low - cane lee - nah lee - fah air - lie Eel dills
Low - tim - jay-rt Eel low - pay – tune."

**FAERIE BLESSING SPELL:** (Faeries can curse but they'd rather give blessings. Wouldn't you? Let all who see you in this garment be blest.)
**"How lucky you are that you do see**
**The passing by of this faerie."**

(Arvyndase)

**"Po nivath le da dij le ba ten
Tae goldas la u wyr farri."**

(Pronunciation)
"Poe nigh - vayth lee dah dye-j lee bah teen
Tay goal - dace lah you were fair – rye."

**FAERIE GLAMOR SPELL:** (Faeries are perhaps best noted for their glamor spells. This is rather like the enchantment spell but with a bit of extra sparkle added.)
**"Glittering brightly like a star
All can see me from afar."**

(Arvyndase)
**"Lumyrtdas ilula sylar na mêl
Wyl vek ten el an narlo."**

(Pronunciation)
Lou - mert - dace eye - lou - lah sill - lair nah mell
Will veek teen eel ane nair – low.

༄

"Surely the shine of the elven is somewhat diminished by contact with the world, but it is also true that we have infected the world with our magic at the same time, leaving sparkles of shimmering elvishness wherever we go."

"We are a dream of tomorrow's rememberings and yesterday's visions combined, dancing around the fire eternal the magic of Elfin we find."

# Chapter 2 . . . . Headdresses, Crowns, Tiaras, & Circlets

**Zardoa in his Elven Owl Brothers Headdress.**
Instructions for creating this headdress are in the following pages.

We love to make crowns, tiaras, circlets, head dresses and other artifacts of magic as head adornments to go with our elven costumes. These are not the usual crowns of kings or queens (although they are surely fit for elven royalty) but are more of a ritualistic piece of hair jewelry imbued with elven magic spell crafting.

**The Magical Image:** *A jeweled tiara with beautiful peacock feathers dangling from the band adorns the brow of the elven princess and casts a spell of enchantment upon all whom she greets.*

## Materials to Collect:

For our crowns and headwear, we collect all manner of magically interesting natural pieces and materials, including feathers, shells, bones, antlers, small pieces of wood in interesting shapes, and even skulls of small birds or animals we have found in nature or even on occasion as road kill. These natural materials are useful in making all sorts of magical artifacts like staffs and wands and also elven crowns. So it is that we elves collect all such natural materials that come to us. We have also used materials that are not found directly in nature or have been processed somewhat, including painted beads, broken jewelry, small smooth stones, silk, satin and velvet strips of cloth, and many other interesting pieces our intuitions said to save that we found, bought at second hand stores, or was given to us. We place all of these pieces on our magic tables and they may stay there for years, having spells and elven blessings placed upon them daily. Eventually, it will come to us either in a dream or through our intuition that certain of these pieces are suppose to go together for a particular magical artifact such as a crown and then we proceed to make it.

We will give you an example in the directions below of a head dress that we very recently made using two items we had for many years: 1.) a group of feathers sewn together in a sort of toupee that we found years ago at a yard sale, and 2.) the skull of an owl that had met with a tragic car accident and we found on the side of the road 10 or more years ago.

## Directions:

One day, Zardoa was playing around with the feathered toupee mentioned above, jokingly putting it on his head to make a happy birthday video for our elven grandson in Ukraine, Nikolay Lyapenkenko, who had just turned 15 years old. The feather toupee had been in among our magic for over 30 years, but we had never had a vision of it being used for an artifact. The next day, Zardoa had an insight that the toupee could be embellished to be a magical headdress. So he placed a small owl skull on the top part of the toupee (see the photo on the next page that is on the left). Then he could easily visualize braided yarn dangling down off of it, like braids of hair, as a sort of headdress. So he wove some yarn into two double braids the same length. We suggest a thick yarn, by the way, for this project. Our yarn was a light color and Zardoa thought it would look better if it was a brown color, matching the feathers. So he soaked the braids in a combination of coffee grounds and Assam black tea grounds (which we make chai from each morning) and water (see the photo below on the right) over night and then hung them to dry. Naturally, these were used grounds, we weren't about to waste good coffee or tea, this is hedgewitchery, after all. Next he wrapped colored embroidery thread around the bottom and the top of each of the braids.

**Left: Owl skull on toupee Right: Soaking woven yarn in coffee grounds, black tea grounds & water to dye brown.**

The final step was for him to attach the braids, hanging down from the sides of the skull (see photo at the beginning of this chapter of Zardoa modeling his Owl Brothers elven headdress).

Of course, we also enjoy making simple crowns and tiaras to match our costumes and these are rather easy to make compared to our headdresses. We simply use a premade headband (see the photo on the left of the inexpensive wire and plastic ones found in discount department stores) and we use tacky glue or Sobo glue to glue on jewels (mostly collected from our broken jewelry collection), sequins, feathers and sometimes small stones or gems. Just let your imagination be your guide. Below is a photo of one we made just yesterday:

**Simple elven crown.**

And of course you may also wish to make a more elaborate crown, using a simple headband as a base. After finding a main crown piece that you think would make a great crown ornament, there are a few simple steps more. Here is how we made the Elven Leaf Crown shown in the photos on the next page:

1.    We took a beautiful found ornament we thought would make a perfect crown and painted it with 'gold leaf' (comes in sheets and can be bought at an art store), leaving some areas showing black underneath. We were not sure what this piece was originally as we found it at a garage sale, but our elven brother Michael Leo Periard, of the Universal Elven Society, made a similar crown and has told us that it is from a realm of a bike helmet.

2.    Next, after the crown piece dried overnight, we glued cloth leaves onto the back of the crown piece (shown on the left in the photo on the following page).

3.    We glued a jewelry piece (an old single earring we had in our treasures) on the front center of the ornament (shown on the right in the photo on the following page).

4.    Then we glued the two ties (any thick string will do) so that they were on the outside of the headband. The string is glued all the way around the outside of the headband for strength.

5.    The last step is to glue the crown piece with the leaves on it onto the headband, folding the leaves under on the bottom and gluing them to the inside of the headband.

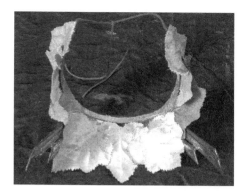
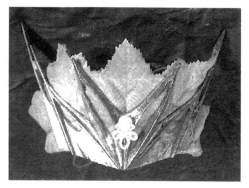

Here in the photo below is Zardoa modeling the Elven Leaf crown. You will notice in the background some diplomas on the wall. These are some of our magical diplomas and we shall get to how to make those in a later chapter.

We have also made other simple crowns using cloth, lace, yarn and feathers and other pieces that we intuitively felt would fit together. Often, we saved interesting bits of these materials for years before the crown idea using them came to us. One of our favorite crowns is the Elven Feather Boa Crown. We cut the main headband cloth piece form a Jughead hat (the style of hat that the character Jughead wore in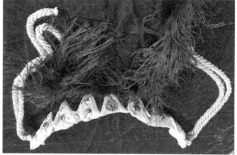
the original Archey comics) and decorated it with old jewelry. The feathers are from an old rather broken up feather boa someone discarded and we saved for years before realizing it would be beautiful as a major part of this crown. The boa is sewn across the inside of the

band so that the two ends dangle out in equal measure and may be worn as Zardoa models in the photo below:

**Zardoa in Elven Feather Boa Crown**

Also here shown on the right is a photo of a lacy crown that Silver Flame models. The main piece of this lacy crown was something we found in a free box on a table at a garage sale. We have no idea of its original purpose. But it looked interesting to us and we thought right off that it might make a great crown. So we took it home and made one of our very first crowns. It is a very beautiful crown and all we had to do was to tie on some lace ribbons on each side in the back for attaching to ones head, showing that much elven art and hedgewitchy is in the magic of collecting found items. Since all elves are royal, it is perfectly acceptable for all elves to wear crowns. And now for some spell casting for all ye crowned elf witches.

## Elven Spell Casting

**NOBILITY SPELL:** (Note: you can say faerie instead of elven, or whatever you choose or may happen to be, such as noble werewolf or whatever.)
**"Noble elven to the core**
**The Pride of those who came before."**

(Arvyndase)
**"Eldae êldata va tae dor
Tae Rosk u dijli jae kosoïn lokan."**

(Pronunciation)
Eel - day l - day - tah vah tay door
Tay Rowsk you dye-j - lie jay co - so - in low - cane.


ENCHANTMENT SPELL:
**"Crowned I am in elven glory
The Reality am I of Faerie Story."**

(Arvyndase)
**"Julonïn El da ver êldata foma
Tae Althtu da El u Farri Molfa."**

(Pronunciation)
Jew - lone - in Eel dah veer l - day - tah foe - mah
Tay Ale-th - two dah Eel you Fair - rye Mole – fah.


ASPIRATION SPELL: (Since the third eye resides at the 'crown' chakra, the jewel in the crown represents higher aspiration and the jewel in the crown is the third eye.)
**"Ever upward I ascend
To the great heights where elven tend."**

(Arvyndase)
**"Vari repvur El rystar
Va tae ralt altarli ern êldata lert."**

(Pronunciation)
Vay - rye reap - viewer Eel riss - tayr
Vah tay rail-t ale - tayr - lie ear-n l - day - tah leer-t.


ILLUMINATION SPELL: (Again, because the jewel in the crown indicates the third eye, the crown indicates one's power to spread light and enlightenment into the world.)
**"Bright the light that from me beams
The truth revealed beyond what seems."**

(Arvyndase)
**"Ilu tae lun dij an el drynlu
Tae lodver sotosïn hyrlon wu kacerlu."**

(Pronunciation)
Eye - lou tay loon dye-j ane eel dryn - lou
Tay load - veer so - toe-ss - in her - lone woo kay - sir – lou.

**HEALING SPELL:** (Traditionally a king or monarch had the power of healing as a sign of being the true king, as per example Aragorn in *the Return of the King.*)
**"From my eyes light doth spread**
**And every ill is quickly shed."**

(Arvyndase)
**"An el'na arli lun båver wyd**
**Nar lotym nål da zifla jors."**

(Pronunciation)
Ane eel'nah air - lie loon bah - veer wid
Nair low - tim nahl dah zief - lah jours.

**"The Path to Elfin begins in one's soul,**
**one's urge to be loving,**
**find kin and be whole,**
**it moves through one's mind,**
**one's imagination awakes,**
**magic then swirling as the first step one takes."**
**—Wisdom of the Elders**

**"The Elves Say: Some people wonder why we elves seem lost in the world search for Elfin everywhere, but remember, this is just a game of hide and seek."**

**"You can search for what seems like forever to Elfin and never find it.**
**You can wait for it to come and it never seems to arrive.**
**But if you live the life Elfin, it emerges all around you like buds in the springtime."**
**—Old Elven Saying**

# Chapter 3 . . . . Elven Banner Art (Sewn)

We love making magical banners and have done so in both the virtual world using Illustrator as a graphics program and also sewing them and/or painting them on satin or cotton material. Later in this book, we will show you a few examples of virtual banners and talk about the process of making them, but in this chapter we will be looking at the ones we have sewn or painted on cloth. An elven banner is much like an Elfin flag and we always have liked to hang them on our tents at magical gatherings and also in our eald (Elven home). Below is one of our favorite Silver Elves banners hanging in our eald:

**Note:** If you have taken our 'What Kind of Elf, Fae, or Otherkin Are You? What is Your Tribe?' questionnaire (and if you have not and would like to do so, then please see our website at http://silverelves.angelfire.com/HAelfkin.html), then you find that we ask you a number of questions that will help us identify what your particular elfae tribe banner looks like (like favorite colors, animal totem, flower, magical symbols, etc), and we often describe it and explain the importance of it to your tribe in the narrative that we gift you.

**The Magical Image:** *The elves busily stitch their magic into a beautiful banner to adorn their eald.*

## Materials Needed:

Begin by collecting cloth that is at least three feet across and four feet in length. This will be for the main background and we suggest it to be a solid color. Satins work well. You will also need cloth of different colors to use for cutting symbols to sew on the background, marking chalk, thread and needles, and scissors.

## Directions:

You first need to think about what your banner is going to represent. Draw out on paper the symbols you would like on your banner. You may wish to consult our *The Book of Elven Runes* for rune symbols to use and also create some symbols yourself. We often use the 7-pointed elf star and some astrological symbols relating to the theme of the banner. Also think about what shape you would like the banner itself. Once you decide on the basic shape of the banner, we suggest that you chalk it out on the banner before cutting. We suggest three feet wide and four feet long, but you may feel industrious and wish for one much larger. Since we like to hang ours up in our home, this is a perfect size for our small apartment yet large enough to display at magical gatherings. Remember to leave about ½ inch all around the edge so you can iron it under and sew a hem. Once you have drawn it, cut it out, and sewn down the seams, then you are ready to make the symbols to put on the banner.

After drawing out the symbols, you are ready to cut the extra material into symbols and place them on the background cloth that you have selected and prepared. It works well to also have a seam edge that you can fold under all around the symbols and iron down. Once you have placed the symbols where you would like them, pin them and finish by sewing them on the banner. Here on the right is an example of a banner that we have made and hung in our elven home or used to decorate our tent at elven-faerie gatherings. It is actually one of our first banners that we made in 1986, and we sometimes still hang it in our eald today. A red heart lays over the symbol of Mercury combined with the glyphs for Venus and Mars, or the intelligent combination of the male and female principles, the active and beautiful together focusing energy toward acting with elegance and intelligence, used in a loving and compassionate way. We also have dangled a quartz crystal on a string from the heart to help stabilize the energy (although it is difficult to see well in this photo). Each symbol and glyph is made of satin, cut with ¼ inch folded over as in a rolled edge. This banner was stitched completely by elven hands, casting our elven spells upon it all the while.

And here to the left we have an example of another banner that we painted on a large cotton cloth to use as a magical triangle for the evocation of spirits in elven ceremonial magick. Instead of painting the triangle and its sigils and glyphs upon the ground, or drawing it there in chalk or with salt, flour or some other substance, we created a movable magical triangle that can be taken from place to place and put down anywhere. The writing around the outside is in one style of Arvyndase script and the inside in another Arvyndase script. (See our book *Arvyndase (Silverspeech): A Short Course in the Magical Language of the Silver Elves.*)

The triangle is filled in with gold paint and in the center of it is another triangle (painted up-side-down) in silver paint (again, difficult to see in this black and white photo but you can see the impression of a flat line going across the outer triangle from one trident like glyph to the other). The two triangles represent a magical triangle for the evocation of spirits. The triangle being a three in numerology is used as a doorway for spirits to enter our world.

We wrote magic scripts for spell casting using our magical language Arvyndase as noted earlier, and the seven-pointed elven stars in each of the four corners. Each elf star has elven spirit signatures written behind them that we drew from our book *An Elfin Book of Spirits*. The three larger symbols are: 1. The elven rune "Iron" (on the bottom) for strength from our book *The Book of Elven Runes*; 2. A Norse rune "Algiz" for protection (on the left) and an elven spirit (on the right) also from our *An Elfin Book of Spirits*.

## Elven Spell Casting

**PROTECTION SPELL**: (to help and protect one's kindred)
**"Secure the people ever be**
**Protected, safe and ever free."**

(Arvyndase)
**"Yader tae jaltar vari te**
**Kafaïn, del nar vari alo."**

(Pronunciation)
Yeah - deer tay jail - tayr vay - rye tea
Kay - fah - in, deal nair vay - rye a – low.

**HEALING SPELL:**
**"All who come within our realm**
**Are healed from their toe to helm."**

(Arvyndase)
**"Wyl jae koso enåver eli'na êld**
**Da hyrnïn an tam'na fof va varl."**

(Pronunciation)
Will jay co - so e - nah - veer e - lie - nah eald
Dah herne - in ane tame'nah foe-f vah vayr-l.

**ENCHANTMENT SPELL:** (Used so that others can see how marvelous your kindred truly are. Only, of course, if you wish to be noticed.)
**"We're here, we're grand, and wondrous proud**
**We stand out in every crowd."**

(Arvyndase)
**"Eli'da jän, eli'da torni, nar tyltålsey ronsk**
**Eli lotz zes ver lotym pylro."**

(Pronunciation)
E - lie'dah jan, e - lie'dah tour - nigh, nair till - tahl - say roan-sk
E - lie lote-z zees veer low - tim pill – row.

**ABUNDANCE SPELL:**
**"Fortune favors all our tribe**
**Luck anointed by destiny's scribe."**

(Arvyndase)
**"Tukor kanilu wyl eli'na êlva**
**Niv sacrylïn la lawath'na nalri."**

(Pronunciation)
Two - core kay - nigh - lou will e - lie'nah l - vah
Nive say - krill - in lah lay - wayth - nah nail – rye.

**GATHERING SPELL:**
**"Come to us, oh, kindred true**
**You're one of ours, our very crew."**

(Arvyndase)
**"Koso va eli, tra, eldivu lod**
**Le'da ata u eli'na, eli lefa chen."**

(Pronunciation)
Co - so vah e - lie, trah, eel - dye - view load
Lee'dah a - tah you e - lie'nah, e - lie lee - fah cheen.

"The Elves Say: Every house and building in Elfin is unique, each with its own architectural beauty and grace, much like the elves thems'elves."

"Elves don't speak of being of the same flesh and blood but of the same soul and spirit."

"We elves never really say goodbye, because in our hearts we know we will surely see our kindred again in this lifetime or another."
—Ancient Elven Wisdom

"If you wish to know of the fae, think of aboriginal peoples around the world in their most spiritual and magical manifestation. Beat the drum and dance. Shake your rattle and chant. Elfin is all about us. Look and see. Can you see the ancient fires burning?"
—Reflections on Elfin

"There are those who say that we elves don't have blood in our bodies but rather magic pulsing though our veins and in a spiritual sense, this is quite true."

# Chapter 4 . . . . Elven Digital Art

These elves love digital graphic arts and find every excuse possible to play with color and image in that form. If you also enjoy making art on your computer, we hope this section will give you some ideas of how you can further use this art form to enhance your magic. We will share with you a few of the ways we use digital art in our magic — our elf dollars, graphic art banners, diplomas of magical accomplishments, and elven blessing labels for candle magic. Let your imagination go wild!

## Elf Dollars

We love to make our own elf dollars or elf kisses for the United Realms of Elfin. Yes, we elves do love to play, so it is no surprise that we like "play money." But our elf kisses are also legal tender and as real as any other dollar bill. On the next page you will see an example of a 100 elf bill on the left that is guaranteed good for 100 kisses (note that the front of bill is pictured on the bottom and the back is on the top); on the right side is an elf bill for 500 kisses. These are made digitally in Illustrator, but Photoshop or any graphic program will work for you. Of course, these are printed in a variety of colors but, alas to keep the cost of the book reasonable, we could only show you them here in black and white.

If you want to view an example of our 100 kiss bill in color and even download and print it for free, we invite you to our silver elves website at http://silverelves.angelfire.com. Just scroll down on our index page and you will find them. Print as much as you need! When you design your own elf dollars, just be sure to add this statement on one side of each bill: "This note is Legal tender and consensual for affairs public and private."

We also add on our bills the date the series was made and issued by the Silver Elves and our web address at the time. You may enjoy decorating your elf kiss (or whatever you call your money) bills with some of your own favorite symbols of good luck and magic. We particularly like to have images of trees on all our elf kiss bills because they are precious to elves in Elfland, like gold is in the world of "normal" folk. We've been known to gift these elf dollars/kisses at magic gatherings; and, in the past when we printed, bound and distributed our books ours'elves, and sent an elven brother or sister a Silver Elves book, we generally always included elf dollars as they make great bookmarks.

Of course, Elven money, such as our Elf Kisses, has little value in the world of Men. However, their true value is in terms of magic. They are enchanting and spell imbued and can be used to spread one's enchantments about the world. Give generously of your elf money and let your spells flow into the world unobstructed, bringing a bit of light, joy and art into the world.

**The Magical Image**: *Elves dance through the crowd of faerie folk generously gifting elf kisses.*

Elf Dollars (Left: 100 kisses, back and front; Right: 500 kisses, back and front).

## Elven Spell Casting

**ABUNDANCE SPELL**: (Obviously used to draw money to you in whatever currency is accepted in your particular country.)
**"Every kiss (or whatever you name your elf or faerie money) doth bring to me Abundance and prosperity."**

(Arvyndase)
**"Lotym mel båver cura va el Konåkora nar doreltu."**

(Pronunciation)
Low - tim meal bah - veer cur - rah vah eel
Co - nah - co - rah nair door - real – two.

**CONNECTION SPELL**: (Money is often a means of connecting with others. Be generous and draw others to you.)
**"I give to you most generously To ease the way between you and me."**

(Arvyndase)
**"El luth va le erst freåmåla**
**Va ham tae yer vyrlan le nar el."**

(Pronunciation)
Eel lewth vah lee ear-st free - ah -mah - lah
Vah haym tay year ver - lane lee nair eel.

**SECURITY SPELL:** (Money isn't just about success in the world, at its base it is about safety and security)
**"All we need does come to us**
**Easily and without fuss."**

(Arvyndase)
**"Wyl eli zanti ba koso va eli**
**Hamla nar enåkon bost."**

(Pronunciation)
Will - e - lie zane - tie bah co - so vah e - lie
Haym - lah nair e - nah - cone boast.

**SUCCESS SPELL:** (While success is about abundance, money also represents success in the world, the ability to make progress and get what you need for continuing on the path. Elven Kisses may not directly buy you things, but if you use them well, and enchant them with magic, their mystic powers will draw to you the things you need.)
**"It comes, bringing success**
**And we proceed upon the quest."**

(Arvyndase)
**"Ter koso, curådas reda**
**Nar eli murfan repton tae ast."**

(Pronunciation)
Tier co - so, cur - rah - dace ree - dah
Nair e - lie muir - fane reap - tone tay ace-t.

## Elf Banners (Graphic)

We have demonstrated in a previous chapter how to sew elf banners out of cloth, but another way to express your elven identity is through digital banners that you may print and frame for your walls in your eald, use as a banner in your magic circle for calling the spirits or for giving elven blessings, or to print and paste as an image for a cover on a dream journal or book of shadows.

First identify the theme for your banner and then, using your favorite graphic arts program, collect all the symbols you wish to use in your banner. You will need to outline the basic shape of the banner and then begin filling it in with the symbols. Because you are making your banner digitally, you have the opportunity to also use some elven runes, spirits, or Arvyndase Silverspeech script to call forth your magic intentions or use Tolkien's elvish scripts, which are quite nice and evocative. Our elf brother Änådae used to send us elf letters addressed in English but using the elvish script style that one sees on the writing of the One Ring. It was really quite nice and a lot of fun.

The digital banner (see the photos below) on the left is an example of one we scripted using elven runes (see our book *The Book of Elven Runes*) to call forth blessings for our dwarf brothers and sisters. We made this banner so it could be printed in its full color, placed in a picture frame and gifted to our dwarf kin to hang on their wall at the entrance of their home for good luck and friendship.

On the right (photo below) is an example of a banner we made to use on a cover for one of Silver Flame's book of shadows. The bee and butterfly are her insect totems that she has found to be helpful for being in touch with her magical healing heritage. So, because this particular book of shadows dealt with recording the performing of healing magic in her dreams, she choose these insect symbols for the banner. In the next chapter we will be looking at how to make elven magical books of shadows. We have also used these graphic banners in one of our elven tarot decks (see Chapter 17 on making tarot decks).

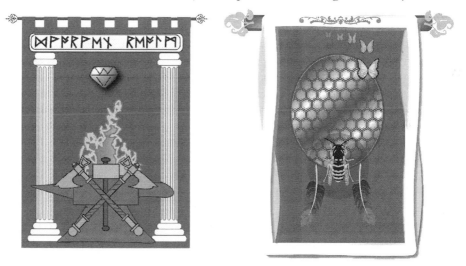

**Left: Blessings for the Dwarves in Silver Elves Runes; Right: Bee and Butterfly.**

**The Magical Image:** *The elven sorcerer uses her insect totems (see below) to recall her magical knowledge of healing through the images in hir dreams.*

## Elven Spell Casting

Depending upon why you create your banner, you may wish to use any of the following spells or a combination thereof. But, it is also possible to have purposes other than the ones covered here so always feel free to create your own spells.

**DESTINY SPELL:**
**"Our people call us from the stars**
**A future bright shall soon be ours."**

(Arvyndase)
**"Eli'na jaltar koar eli an tae mêlli**
**Na lasel ilu van qun te eli'na."**

(Pronunciation)
E - lie'nah jail - tayr co - air e - lie ane tay mell - lie
Nah lay - seal eye - lou vane que-n tea e - lie'nah.

**INDIVIDUATION SPELL:**
**"Bright our banner, noble, proud**
**Great our people, say it loud."**

(Arvyndase)
**"Ilu eli'na corylon, eldae, ronsk**
**Ralt eli'na jaltar, des ter ruol."**

(Pronunciation)
Eye - lou e - lie'nah core - rill - lone, eel - day, roan-sk
Rail-t e - lie'nah jail - tayr, deece tier rue – ole.

**ABUNDANCE SPELL:**
**"Fortune swiftly doth arrive**
**And thus our people ever thrive."**

(Arvyndase)
**"Tukor vysla båver komal**
**Nar hern eli'na jaltar vari dorv."**

(Pronunciation)
Two - core viss - lah bah - veer co - male
Nair hear-n e - lie'nah jail - tayr vay - rye door-v.

**HEALING SPELL:**
**"Healing comes to those who see**
**Our banner proud and flying free."**

(Arvyndase)
**"Hyrndas kosolu va dijli jae ten**
**Eli'na corylon ronsk nar fosdas alo."**

(Pronunciation)
Herne - dace co - so - lou vah dij - lie jay teen
E - lie'nah core - rill - lone roan-sk nair foe-ss - dace a – low.

**MAGIC ENHANCEMENT SPELL:** (to enhance the power of your magic in your eald or wherever you may be hanging or flying your banner)

**"Our magic power doth greatly grow**
**As our banner each comes to know."**

(Arvyndase)
**"Eli'na êldon eldro båver raltla lyth**
**Tat eli'na corylon cha kosolu va ken."**

(Pronunciation)
E - lie'nah l - doan eel - drow bah - veer rail-t - lah lith
Tate e - lie'nah core - rill - lone chah co - so - lu vah keen.

**GATHERING SPELL:**
**"To our banner our people come**
**Strong together, we stand as One."**

(Arvyndase)
**"Va eli'na corylon eli'na jaltar koso**
**Mylth eldan, eli lotz tat Ata."**

(Pronunciation)
Vah e - lie'nah core - rill - lone e - lie'nah co - so
Mill-th eel - dane, e - lie lote-z tate A – tah.

## Magic Studies Diplomas

We love to make diplomas for the magical accomplishments of both our kin and ourselves and then hang them on our wall that we call the Hall of Magic. (Sometimes we refer to our home as a museum of elven and faerie art, lore and culture.) While we hold a number of graduate degrees that were accompanied by well-designed official diplomas, these never make our wall and in fact they are all sitting inside a box collecting dust under our bed with other storage items. For it is the accomplishment of magic studies and efforts that we cherish the most in our experience and for these we enjoy adopting a similar look to an official diploma to celebrate that which is of true value to us. And we have translated our worldly diplomas, the one's we've achieved in the world, into magic diplomas as though we had gone to Hogwarts or Brakebills or some other magical academy, for while we did study in worldly institutions, being magically minded it was still magic that we were studying and learned. We simply asked ours'elves, if we have gotten this degree at Brakebills (from Lev Grossman's *The Magician* trilogy and TV series), for instance, what would it say.

Our magic studies diplomas are made digitally in either Illustrator or Photoshop. Of course, you can use any graphic program you wish and experiment with a variety of fonts and frames for your creations. Have some fun with this! We elves use this art as both an exercise in developing one's sense of humor and in honoring what is truly important to us. Below are a couple of examples of our diplomas and certificates in our Hall of Magic:

Left: Zardoa's 8th degree magician certificate from Linton Hall Academy of Magic
Right: Zaroda's advanced Master of Arts diploma in enchanted sorcery.

**The Magical Image:** *A wizard hands out diplomas to graduating magicians.*

## Elven Spell Casting

**RECOGNITION SPELL:** (In many ways diplomas are a recognition of your efforts and accomplishments. You deserve to be recognized for what you have done. This spell serves to bring that recognition to you.)

**"Now comes to me all credit earned
I'm lauded now and never spurned."**

(Arvyndase)
**"Mat kosolu va el wyl dothal orfïn**
**El'da trosïn mat nar konzar rutïn."**

(Pronunciation)
Mate co - so - lou vah eel will doe - thayl orf - in
Eel'dah trowce - in mate nair cone - zair root - in

**KNOWLEDGE SPELL:** (Often achieving a degree is not just about graduating but a recognition of a greater ability to learn on a higher level of development. With this spell, all you need to know, all the information, facts and inspiration that you desire will come to you.)
**"What I need to know revealed**
**In every way and every field."**

(Arvyndase)
**"Wu El golt va ken sotosïn**
**Ver lotym yer nar lotym kolan."**

(Pronunciation)
Woo Eel goal-t vah keen so - toe-ss - in
Veer low - tim year nair low - tim co – lane.

**ACHIEVEMENT SPELL:** (A diploma is a recognition of achievement but also is meant to open the way to greater success in the world and, as far as magic goes, on the various planes and dimensions. This spell fosters your future success and progress.)
**"This is the start I now begin**
**From here now onward I ascend."**

(Arvyndase)
**"Wyr da tae altu El mat cysyl**
**An jän mat gosvur El rystar."**

(Pronunciation)
Were dah tay ale - two Eel mate sis - sill
Ane jan mate gos - viewer Eel riss – tayr.

**ASCENSION SPELL:** (To graduate is to move to a higher level of manifestation. This is especially true for magical diplomas. This spell will help you evolve and ascend ever higher upon your path of magic and enchantment.)
**"Ever higher I do rise**
**Greater realms to realize."**

(Arvyndase)
**"Vari altfa El ba luft
Raltfa êldli va althna."**

(Pronunciation)
Vay - rye ale-t - fah Eel bah lew-ft
Rail-t - fah eald - lie vah ale-th – nah.

## Labels for Magic Candles

We Silver Elves have a fondness for candle burning and find tall votive candles that come in glass cylinders to be particularly good for this magic. Such candles are available at most grocery stores, although many of them have various Christian saints or prayers to Jesus upon them and while we think Jesus was a wonderful elf and magician, we prefer more magically inclined candles for spell working. Of course, you can buy these more magical votive candles at some metaphysical shops but we, being the elven hedgewitches that we are, enjoy making our own labels according to our particular needs, desires and magical aspirations and then pasting them to our candles.

**The Magical Image:** *Elves sit in meditative silence around a candle with an elven spell for healing a sister elf.*

## Materials to Collect:

There is not much to it really. Get some tall, glass votive candles. Make your spell label. You can use Photoshop or Illustrator or some other graphics program. But you can also collect images and make a collage, or simply draw your own. And a bit of glue will be needed to paste on your new label. It's that easy.

## Directions:

Most likely you will have to buy the votive candles yours'elf. If you buy ones that are already spell cast from metaphysical shops they will probably be really expensive. This is part of the reason we make our own, but also, we just like to do our own enchanting. Regular shops often have these type candles, but we've found that if there is a local grocery store dedicated to Mexican food, you will probably find them to be less expensive there.

It is sometimes possible to find plain glass candles, and that would surely be best, but most are either printed on or have a label honoring Jesus, Mary, or sometimes success at the lotto, which you just may wish to keep as is.

Once you have created your label in Illustrator or Photoshop or drawn one yours'elf or collaged one from pictures you've gathered that suggest the magic you are interested in promoting, you may wish to add a word or two in large type to it, like ABUNDANCE or HEALING, etc. that identifies the intention of the candle. Generally a label for a tall votive candle would be about three inches by four inches in dimension. You can also add a spirit sigil from our book *An Elfin Book of Spirits* or one of our Elven Runes from our book *The Book of Elven Runes* or whatever magical tradition you feel kinship toward.

Here are two candle labels we created also using runes from our *The Book of Elven Runes*:
Left: To bring us **Greater Wisdom**; Right: To bring us **Longevity**.

If the candle is blank, that's great. If it is printed on, you may wish to scrape off the old printing and picture and paste your label over it, or just go ahead and paste it over. But if it already has a label, you probably wish to steam off the old label, magically removing any spell already associated with it at the same time, before gluing the new one on. Don't forget to do a spell and enchant your candle as desired.

## Elven Spell Casting

The number of possible spell intentions for candles is vast. But on the following page we have some of the most likely and common ones.

**ABUNDANCE SPELL:**
"Money comes, and money goes
But to me money ever flows."

(Arvyndase)
**Latenth kosolu, nar latenth taslu
Kana va el latenth vari shurlu."**

(Pronunciation)
Lay-teenth co - so - lou, nair lay-teenth tace - lou
Kay - nah vah eel lay-teenth vay - rye sure – lou.


**HEALING SPELL:**
"Healing from the inside out
Healing magic all about."

(Arvyndase)
**Hyrndas an tae verfålaten zes
Hyrndas êldon wyl basar."**

(Pronunciation)
Herne - dace ane tay veer - fah - lay - teen zees
Herne - dace l - doan will bay – sayr.

**HEALING SPELL:** (especially for healing others)
"By my will you are now healed
To healing's way you ever yield."

(Arvyndase)
**La eli'na yon le da mat hyrnïn
Va hyrndas'na yer le vari ped."**

(Pronunciation)
Lah - e - lie'nah yone lee dah mate herne - in
Vah herne - das'nah year lee vay - rye peed.

**SUCCESS SPELL:**
"Success is mine, the time is right
And comes to me by magic rite."

(Arvyndase)
**"Reda da el'na, tae mern da mard**
**Nar kosolu va el la êldon mår."**

(Pronunciation)
Ree - dah dah eel'nah, tay mere-n dah mare-d
Nair co - so - lou vah eel lah l - doan mar.

**MAGIC SPELL:** (to increase your magical powers)
**"Magic power within me grows**
**From my head down to my toes."**

(Arvyndase)
**"Êldon eldro enåver el lythlu**
**An el'na dim dab va el'na fofli."**

(Pronunciation)
L - doan eel - drow [rhymes with row] e - nah - veer eel lyth - lou
Ane eel'nah dime dayb vah eel'nah foe-f – lie.

**KNOWLEDGE SPELL:**
**"Secrets great revealed to me**
**And all my powers are set free."**

(Arvyndase)
**"Marynli ralt sotosïn va el**
**Nar wyl el'na eldroli da pånd alo."**

(Pronunciation)
May - ren - lie rail-t so - toe-ss - in vah eel
Nair will eel'nah eel - drow - lie dah pond a – low.

**LOVE SPELL:**
**"Draw to me those I adore**
**Who for their part adore me more."**

(Arvyndase)
**"Omhyr va el dijli El radiåten**
**Jae fro tam'na sun radiåten el gilf."**

(Pronunciation)
Om - her vah eel dye-j - lie Eel ray - dye - ah - teen
Jay fro tame'nah soon ray - dye - ah - teen eel gile-f.


**HAPPINESS SPELL:**
**"Joyous now is each day**
**Happiness comes in every way."**

(Arvyndase)
**"Elsåsey mat da cha lea**
**Ejartu kosolu ver lotym yer."**

(Pronunciation)
Eel - sah - say mate dah chah lee - ah
E - jayr - two co - so - lou veer low - tim year.


**SPIRITUAL ADVANCEMENT SPELL:**
**"Ever upward I ascend**
**As greater light doth portend."**

(Arvyndase)
**"Vari repvur El rystar**
**Tat raltfa lun båver imfad."**

(Pronunciation)
Vay - rye reap - viewer Eel riss - tayr
Tate rail-t - fah loon bah - veer I'm — fade.


**SPIRIT SPELL:** (for summoning a particular spirit for a special mission, service or assignment)
**"(Name of spirit you are evoking) you now arrive**
**To fulfill my will you ever strive."**

(Arvyndase)
**"..... le mat komal**
**Va felu el'na yon le vari tru."**

(Pronunciation)
..... lee mate co - male
Vah fee - lou eel'nah yone lee vay - rye true.

**FINDING YOUR TRUE S'ELF SPELL:**
"Increasingly, I come to know
Just who I am the truth to show."


(Arvyndase)
**"Memarnla, El koso va ken
Oda jae El da tae lodver vah teke."**

(Pronunciation)
Me - mare-n - lah, Eel co - so vah keen
Oh - dah jay Eel dah tay load - veer vah tea – key.


**LONGEVITY SPELL:**
"Though I do age, I'll forever be
Youthful in mind, spirit and body."

(Arvyndase)
**"Nåt El ba nan, El'yon varigos te
Tylfverfel ver car, tari nar miwa."**

(Pronunciation)
Knot Eel bah nane, Eel'yone vay - rye - gos tea
Till-f - veer - feel veer car, tay - rye nair my – wah.


**WISDOM SPELL:**
"Understanding comes so clear
I see the future without fear."

(Arvyndase)
**"Nehådas kosolu re vyrn
El ten tae lasel enåkon mak."**

(Pronunciation)
Knee - hah - dace co - so - lou re vern
Eel teen tay lay - seal e - nah - cone make.

# Chapter 5 . . . . Magic Books of Shadows or Grimoire (Books of Twilight)

An elven book of shadows may be used to record all of one's magic. We elves often call them Books of Twilight! This collection might include one's magical rituals, dreams, memories of magical moments and synchronicities, spell casting, oracles including runes, tarot and I-Ching secrets, personal and community astrological information, your own visions, intentions, wish fulfillment, herbal medicines and potions, moon phases information, garden information on planting and how to dry herbs and use them for healing purposes, recipes for celebrations, favorite totem animals photos and descriptions of their powers and gifts along with stories of their visitations with you and magical connections, crystals and properties, past life memories, flower photos and dried specimens, artistic ideas and photos or sketches of ritual art projects and altars, creative ideas for writing, elven Arvyndase script, and anything that relates to living your magic. There is nothing that is "suppose to go" in this book nor that is "not suppose to go" in this book. It is your book and only your book, and its purpose is to house a record of your magic for your use only or to share with your Elven kin.

We have made a number of Books of Shadows throughout the years, including books for our children beginning as early as age ten. Of course, what they put in their books was quite different from what we put in ours. Theirs included descriptions and photos of favorite walks and communing in nature as well as their favorite magical characters in such books and films as *The Lord of the Rings* and *The Hobbit*, and even *Final Fantasy* video game story details and characters. Elvira made her way into one of their books, and we welcomed all of our children's images of their own understanding of their magical life. Whatever the person feels will speak to or of their own magical being and experience of magic is important to include. A Book of Elven Shadows is somewhat like a magical scrapbook.

At the same time, these magic books can be very beautiful. For ours'elves, we love seeing pictures of Magic Books and Books of Shadows on the Internet and in various movies and television shows. We find them to be beautiful and inspiring. Since we have been publishing our writings, these books that we share with you have, in many ways, become our Books of Shadows. Before that we created and still possess three volumes of Books of Shadows that we created by hand that are sitting on a shelf just above us as we type this.

**The Magical Image:** *A Book of Twilight lays open upon a table revealing a spirit sigil while candles burn as an Elf Witch studies it carefully.*

## Materials to Collect:

- PVA, flexible resin Bookbinding glue, don't use regular glue it gives way with moisture and hardens solid. This glue flexes as you open the pages.
- Regular glue, such as Sobo's for gluing velvet or other material on the inside covers.
- All purpose Sealer, for sealing the cover.
- Small stones and crystals
- Colorful yarn
- Beautiful buttons and small shells, sequins, jewelry pieces, and feathers
- Photos of totem animals, of you in magic attire, of your altars and magic circles, photos that inspire you magically
- Color pens, including silver and gold sharpies
- Paint
- Book with blank pages (see directions below)
- Kite string (optional)
- Dremel drill (optional)
- C-clamps
- Lengths of wood flat on each side about an inch or two in width and a foot or more in length, depending on the size of your book. We wrap these wood sections with adhesive tape, because PVA glue won't seal to it and this way you won't glue your pages to the wood clamped on either side to hold the book together when being bound.

## Directions:

We like to find an old ornately decorated encyclopedia, gut the insides, and replace it with our own blank paper. They are usually easy to find at thrift stores and are often given away freely or sold very inexpensively. After gluing the pages, we use the PVA bookbinding glue inside the book  of our own paper that we have cut to the size of the encyclopedia, we decorate the front using gold or silver sharpie pens and coloring in the raised lines (see photo on next page). We often add velvet, very nice, or sometimes canvas or even a nice paper to the inside covers (see photo above with black velvet inside page). This is done with regular glue. For additional strength in binding, we drill five holes (we have a Dremel drill press for this), after initially binding the pages together, from side to side and weave kite string between them. This makes the binding extra strong. Then we use PVA glue again and glue the pages to canvas we have glued to the inside of the cover. This is before we add velvet to the back and front inside of the covers.

**Zardoa's three volumes of his book of shadows made from old encyclopedias and decorated by using gold or silver sharpie pens and coloring in the raised lines.**

Of course, you may also wish to just buy a plain notebook and decorate the front of it. Collect materials to decorate the front cover like: sequins, small stones and crystals, shells, broken jewelry, feathers you have found on walks in nature, other small found objects of magical significance, colorful yarn, and photos of your totem animals or other magical connections. You will also need color pens and a glue gun to fasten the decorations onto your cover. Of course, you can just draw or paint a beautiful picture and paste it on the front (on the right, see the graphic of a

bee with honey comb that Silver Flame created in Illustator and placed on her Book of

Shadows to represent her relationship to The Shining Ones). The point is to make it beautiful, magical and enchanting to you! We usually seal the cover with Ceramcoat all purpose sealer. Also, we find it a nice touch to use a gold ink pen that you can find in art supply stores and paint the outer edges of the inside pages, so you see the gold when the book is closed.

We also have made a **"Scrapbook of Shadows"** that was very large and contained representations of all our many magical art processes during a three year period, all of which were a part of a magic we did to create a specific outcome of elfin magic. For elf witches who enjoy scrapbooking, this process is truly enjoyable. To do this, you need to find a very large blank book at an art store. The one we used was 12 inches wide and 14 inches long and had about 50 blank pages. We filled it with photos of our magical art, even samples of our art (for example putting small flat magic rocks, which we had painted our sigils upon, into an envelop and pasting it in the book), written spells, and accounts of our personal magical experiences related to our art during this three year period. So if you do this one, just use all your scrapbooking skills to be creative! Elven covens (the elves call their coven, a vortex) can do this large book of shadows together if desired, filling it as a group effort for a magical group outcome. This is a powerful way to honor your magick, particularly a magick that you are doing over a certain long period of time for a specific important outcome.

For our large Scrapbook of Shadows (above), we Silver Elves used an art process for the cover using colored tissue paper and sealant to make layers. It wasn't intended but the outcome looks like a house at the top with a dragon making a path to it. So we repeated this magical symbol of the dragon by also gluing upon it a piece of jewelry shaped as a dragon.

Here are a few other suggestions for the inside of your Scrapbook of Shadows, just be creative and let your intuition go wilde:

- Use rubber stamps of stars and metaphysical symbols
- Make up a spell using words you have journaled on a page
- Glue an envelope or make your own pocket to a page, hide a very secret, sacred magic
- Attach a ribbon or cord for closing the book
- Add fold-outs like maps and other art made for your magic
- Glue fitting titles in fancy scripts from a magazine to your magic journaling pages
- Use Arvyndase Wizard Script for titles
- Use beads, yarn and beautiful ribbon to lace the outline the edges of pages
- Hang yarns and ribbons from the spine
- Burn the edges of pages when journaling about magic circles using fire as an element

We also wish to add that it is important to decorate and write your name and volume number on the spine of your Book of Shadows and then seal over it. This can be very important in finding them easily when you have a number of them and wish to stack them on a shelf.

**Zardoa's three Books of Shadows stacked on his desk.**

## Elven Spell Casting:

**KNOWLEDGE SPELL:** (A Book of Shadows is not only a journal or diary of your magical workings but is, in a sense, also an enchanted book drawing greater knowledge to you.)
**"Deep the knowledge to me revealed
The Universe does its power yield."**

(Arvyndase)
**"Dorae tae kenvu va el sotosïn
Tae Atålora bålu ter'na eldro ped."**

(Pronunciation)
Door - ray tay keen - view vah - eel so - toe-ss - in
Tay A - tah - lore - rah bah - lou tier'nah eel - drow peed.

**MAGIC SPELL:** (Use to increase the potency of the spells within the book. Think of your Book of Shadows as a kind of cauldron, brewing up and percolating your magic.)
**"The potency of these spells increase
Ever after without surcease."**

(Arvyndase)
**"Tae mamerva u wyrli mojåli memarn
Vari låka enåkon halwal."**

(Pronunciation)
Tay  may - mere - vah you were - lie moe - jah - lie me - mare-n
Vay - rye lah - kay e - nah - cone hail – whale.

**PRIVACY, SECRECY SPELL:** (Use for keeping your Book of Shadows and spells secret from those who are not ready to handle such power.)
**"Deep the power here contained
Where all its secrets shall remain."**

(Arvyndase)
**"Dorae tae eldro jän okturïn
Ern wyl ter'na marynli van atas."**

(Pronunciation)
Door - ray tay eel - drow jan oak - tour - in
Ear-n will tier'nah may - ren - lie vane a – tace.

**ENCHANTMENT SPELL**: (You may not wish to keep your Book of Shadows secret, rather you may wish it to be filled with beauty and art and esoteric knowledge to enchant those who see it.)
**"Illumination and quite bright
Like a star shines through the night."**

(Arvyndase)
**"Tabitreradur nar ven ilu
Sylar na mêl glislu joul tae sol."**

(Pronunciation)
Tay - by - tree - ray - dur nair veen eye - lou
Sill - lair nah mell glice - lou joe - yule tay soul.

**SPELL OF LASTING**: (Use so your Book of Shadows and your magic will be passed down to future generations!)
**"Through the ages long endure
These spells passed on forevermore."**

(Arvyndase)
**"Joul tae nanli tiso talos
Wyrli mojåli golïn gos varigostu."**

(Pronunciation)
Joe - yule tay nane - lie tie - so tay - lowce
Were - lie moe - jah - lie goal - in go-ss vay - rye - go-ss – two.

**GRAMMARYE SPELL**: (Sometimes writing a spell in a Grimoire is also a process of spell casting. This is seen in movies like the Japanese *Death Note* series where the owner writes in his Death Note Grimoire and causes a person's death on the date and time and in the fashion he writes down. There are other series as well with a similar notion that what the person writes becomes reality. This is the sub-theme, for instance, of the Supernatural TV series in which God, also known as Chuck, is a writer.)
**"Manifesting what I write
My will achieved in magic's sight."**

(Arvyndase)
**"Arotodas wu Eel kalj
El'na yon melobïn ver êldon'na terad."**

(Pronunciation)
A - row - toe - dace woo Eel kale-j
Eel'nah yone me - lobe - in veer l - doan'nah tea – raid.

74

# Chapter 6 . . . . Making Magic Dolls

The art of doll making has been used in magic since ancient times. Traditionally, when we think of doll making for magic, we think of voodoo dolls used to assert some power over people, African fertility dolls, or perhaps we think of a shamanistic doll for healing. Elven magic always uses magical items, including dolls, as either an expression of one's own personal elven-faerie myth or for bringing intentions of healing magic to someone's life.

We use dolls in magic not with the intention of power over others but for healing and enchantment. The elven magician brings forth his/her awareness of the authentic s'Elf within by making a figure as a self-portrait. In graduate school, when we were earning our second Masters degree for each of us, this one in Depth Psychology, we spent a lot of time with one of our professors. Dr. Geri Olson, whose primary interest was in dolls, the history of dolls and the psychological import and meaning of dolls. Numerous times we went with her and some of her undergraduate students to local elementary schools where we would help children make dolls in their classes for special class assignments, such as important women in American history, or whatever they were studying at the time.

Sometimes, the children would send letters afterward thanking us, some of these often saying how much they enjoyed learning to sew and complimenting Zardoa on his elven sartorial sense. Zardoa for this part found that most often he wound up helping boys learn to sew by hand (they were quite eager to do so, often for the first time) and especially how to easily thread a needle, a trick that an elven friend of ours had learned from her Basque aunt. We should say that in our elven home, Zardoa does most of the sewing.

**The Magical Image:** *The Magician heals hirself and hir sisters using a human figure.*

## Materials Needed:

It is best to collect a large assortment of materials to select from in most of your elven creative art processes, and this is certainly true in doll making. We suggest that you collect materials for your doll making projects for a few months, at least, and enjoy this part of the process. Many of the items that you have collected for making magic wishing wands and staffs will also be useful in your collection for doll making. Here are just a few suggestions of what you will need or what will come in handy:

- Pieces of cut fabric of a variety of sizes (best include cotton, silk, wool, satins, felt, velvets and more velvets), with a variety of textures and patterns. (This is the most important item to have in abundance!)
- An iron
- Needles, pins, and thread of all colors
- Thin wire and wire cutters
- Regular fabric glue like Tacky Glue
- Scissors
- Varieties of doll hair that you have bought at a craft store (and also thick wool yarn works as well)
- Acrylic paints and small paint brushes
- A glue gun and glue sticks
- Felt tip fabric pens (often used for faces)
- Nature objects like small shells and feathers and fur scraps
- Leather or cotton cords, ribbons and lace
- Charms
- Various accessories, such as tiny buttons, trinkets, beads, broken jewelry pieces, and tiny toy swords or knives, purses or other doll accessories
- Any items that can be used for a magic pouch, a crown, a robe or cape, or a shield
- Simple patterns for clothes for dolls of a variety of sizes as well as needles and thread and sewing machine, if you use one.
- Any small object that you think might feel like it has value to you or an important memory, i.e., old pins and buttons or other memorabilia
- Small to medium sized muslin cloth undecorated dolls* or you may make your own doll head, arms and legs from polymer clay (or your choice of clay) if you are used to working with it.
- Have a tray or basket to use in holding the materials that you select for your specific doll from all the materials that you have laid out

*We buy our cloth dolls from Homesew.com, but there are a number of other good sources on the Internet. You can buy 5 inch dolls (very good for using with children) or 12 inch ones, which are a perfect size for a mythological doll, very inexpensively and in bulk if you like. Buying a premade cloth doll is very helpful for those who have not had much experience with polymer clay or sewing or stuffing their own dolls.

It is best to use tables to lay out all your materials. And remember that you can also use the floor with bags and boxes of odds and ins that can be hunted through for materials to use like a treasure hunt of the unconscious. The more variety of materials and choices for people, the better as this abundance will enhance ones creativity and intuition.

## Directions:

First set all collected materials out. Take your tray or basket with you and quietly select materials that you want to use for your doll. We suggest that you consider every item that you pick as an aspect of the unconscious. Making a doll is an embodied process and will bring forth what is in the unconscious and it can be very helpful in working out feelings, particularly around identifying and embracing one's personal elven myth. You may also use a doll as a magical ally (as a powerfully embodied teraphim) or to allow the unconscious to speak to you and use that as your intent of empowerment in making the doll. Remember that all art is subjective and this is certainly so of mythological doll making. We enjoy assisting people to make three basic types of magical inner figure dolls: the Ally Doll to help you with your creative projects, the Foretelling Doll to reflect your future and bring forth the knowledge held in your unconscious about your Path, and the Angel or Shining One Doll (or your inner elf or Elfae or Other) to express your inner magical being, the direction you are going on the path and the being you are destined to become.

On the next page, is a photo of an ally doll or inner figure doll that we assisted our sister Vålynsea in making. She felt it held her awareness of her personal magical mythology with a feeling of empowerment through insight and intuition. On the right side is a photo of a doll that Silver Flame made from her unconscious, allowing it to speak to her about her future — a doll of foretelling. It is interesting that her doll is of Japanese culture, as she was not conscious at the time of making the doll that she would be embarking on a move to a more Asian/Polynesian based culture in about two years.

**(Left) Vålynsea with her ally doll; (Right) Silver Flame's Foretelling Doll**

If you are helping a small child or elder to make an inner figure doll, assist them as much as they need, but allow them to make as many choices as possible in the materials used (color of clothing, pattern, accessories). Have them pick what it will look like.

**Here is a beautiful angel inner figure doll made by Michiko Spring, our faerie sister who was an amazing art therapist that shared her magic and art-making with hundreds of children.**

When you are finished making your doll, be sure and have a private dialogue with the doll as an inner figure (could be an imaginal dialogue), treat the doll as a real being. We often ask our dolls who they are and what message or gift they bring us. Be sure and display your doll where you can see it often throughout the day and sit quietly with it. It may take a few days to truly understand whom you have brought forth in your life and what they may foretell about your future.

We have used our dolls in our magic circles to bring forth healing and to call our kin. Place the doll, the image, in the center of your circle or upon your magic table (altar). The doll may be a replication of the embodiment of a specific person you wish to heal, or it may be of a person not present that you wish to draw to you and your tribe. Or it could even represent an unknown person so that you are sending out the call for kinship to those who have not as yet crossed your *path*.

## Elven Spell Casting

With this doll image, we call from within our elven souls the Shining Ones, to assist us in bringing forth the true s'elf, to heal the body and spirit, and to empower and strengthen our good health.

CALLING SPELL: (for creating a doll to call your kindred to you)
**"All my kindred come my way**
**Begins for us, a bright new day."**

(Arvyndase)
**"Wyl el'na eldivu koso el'na yer**
**Cysyllu fro eli, na ilu fae lea."**

(Pronunciation)
Will eel'nah eel - dye - view co - so eel'nah year
Sis - sill - lou fro e - lie, nah eye - lou fae lee – ah.

HEALING SPELL:
**"Through this doll I now heal you**
**So greater health you will accrue."**

(Arvyndase)
**"Joul wyr beba El mat hyrn le**
**Re raltfa hyrnver le yon urnal."**

(Pronunciation)
Joe - yule were bee - bah Eel mate herne lee
Re rail-t - fah herne - veer lee yone your – nail.

The Silver Elves

**COMMUNICATION SPELL:** (Use for communication with the Shining Ones or other spirits and giving them a body to dwell within (teraphim) in your home, in that way much like a temple, church, spirit house, etc. gives a place for a spirit to dwell.)
**"Dwell within this body fair**
**So loving friendship we will share."**

(Arvyndase)
**"Lefwa enåver wyr miwa faer**
**Re kyêlådas edarmar eli yon mati."**

(Pronunciation)
Leaf - wah e - nah - veer were me - wah fay - ear
Re key - l - lah - dace e - dare - mare e - lie yone may – tie.


**FORETELLING SPELL:**
**"The future clear I do now see**
**With ever greater clarity."**

(Arvyndase)
**"Tae lasel vyrn El ba mat ten**
**Ena vari raltfa vyrntu."**

(Pronunciation)
Tay lay - seal vern Eel bah mate teen
E - nah vay - rye rail-t - fah vern – two.

**INVOKING SPELL:** (Use for calling a particular aspect within yours'elf to increase your magic, your understanding, your wisdom and your powers, or whatever qualities that you are interested in improving and making greater within yours'elf.)

**"Absorbing now this quality**
**Ever greater I shall be (now mention the power being invoked such as Wisdom, Healing, Magical Power, Enchantment, etc.)."**

(Arvyndase)
**"Soothdas mat wyr truvar**
**Vari raltfa El van te ....."**

(Pronunciation)
So - oath - dace mate were true - vayr
Vay - rye rail-t - fa Eel vane tea .....

**REDIRECTION SPELL:** (We don't recommend cursing people, since all magic returns to the sender, but you may wish to send certain individuals away from you and yours and toward what will make them better and be enlightening for them. Of course, this often results in them suffering all the karma that they have created in order to progress as soulful spirits, but that is their doing.)

**"Far from me you now feel drawn**
**By forces powerful and strong**
**You'll not resist but eager rush**
**With heart a beating and face aflush (now name the person you wish to willingly go elsewhere)."**

(Arvyndase)
**"Uli an el le mat self omhyrïn**
**La dartli eldrofel nar mylth**
**Le'yon kon onlar kana anlar hars**
**Ena bom na natdas nar fyli nålind ....."**

(Pronunciation)
You - lie ane eel lee mate seal-f om - her - in
Lah dare-t - lie eel - drow - feel nair mill-th
Lee'yone cone ohn - lair kay - nah ane - lair hairs
E - nah bow-m nah nate - dace nair fill - lie nah - lined .....

"If you ask the elves what the greatest magical power is, they will tell you healing, for healing sets everything aright. And if you ask them what healing consists of, they will tell true love, for true love heals all things. And if you ask them what the source of true love is, they will tell you it is the **Divine Magic**, for the **Divine Magic** loves all things and eternally seeks their happiness and fulfillment."

"Most people are seeking their moment in the sun, we elves delight in our time in the shade." —Ole Elven Knowledge

The Elves Say: "Many people seek to view us through the lens of their own limitations, but we elves seek to understand others by virtue of their potentialities."

"We elves don't believe in magic because we are superstitious but because we instinctually have faith in the near infinite nature of the Universe and its potentialities."

# Chapter 7 . . . . Elven Dream Pillows

O ur most powerful magic is often done in the dreaming state, particularly as we dream lucidly and begin to perform magic consciously in our dreams. The first step in lucid dreaming is to begin to listen to our dreams and learn to enjoy dreaming and not to be afraid of our dreams, even our nightmares. We had the opportunity to take a number of classes with the late Dr. Jeremy Taylor, a world renowned Dreamworker and a true elf friend (see his book *Dream Work: Techniques for Discovering the Creative Power in Dreams*). Four things he demonstrated over and over to us were that: 1). All dreams come to us for health and healing (even nightmares are to help us face our inner fears) and that we never have a dream that we cannot handle even if it is difficult; 2). Dreams contain images and symbols that are the language of the soul and unconscious; 3). Dreams always have multiple levels of meaning and always have a message or represent new information for us; and 4). Only the dreamer really knows what the dream means (others can only make suggestions by their interpretations), which is why when doing dream interpretation for others, he always suggested that the person started out by saying, "If this were my dream ...".

Elven dream art, like dream pillows and dream catchers, are created to help us both feel comfortable in our dreaming state (to rest our body and mind fully) and to become lucid/conscious in a dreaming state so we may wield our magic and harness the power of our dreaming to effect the world in manifesting Elfin here on Earth (see our book *Manifesting Elfin*, for answers to questions about *The Elven Way*, which is also another book of ours you may wish to check out). Many indigenous people have used dream art for peaceful sleep and visions during sleep, but what makes our dream art specifically elven is in the materials we use and spells we place on the art (and inside the dream pillows).

We elves love to make and use dream pillows above all other dream art both under our heads as we sleep each night and over our eyes to shut out the moon light (or sunlight when we sleep late, which is nearly always) and give us deeper sleep. It is our intention for the dream pillow to assist us in being lucid while doing our elven magic in our dreams. While it is not something we Silver Elves achieve often, being lucid while doing magic in our dreams is one of the most powerful means of doing magic.

**The Magical Image:** *The elf sleeps with hir magic wand under hir dream pillow, ready to cast hir spell upon dream awakening.*

This is a photo of our Elven Lucid Dreaming Pillow that we stuffed with freshly dried mugwort leaves, lavender flowers, three whole cloves, and devil's claw root, with two drops of rosemary essential oil, and placed a paper with one of our elven runes and an elven spirit drawn upon it to help us in our lucid magical dreaming (see instructions below).

## Materials:

- Cloth for covering of the dream pillow. Be sure it is soft and comfortable for sleeping upon.
- Strips of satin and other soft fabric for stuffing or cotton batting (optional)
- Gathered and dried mugwort, lavender and other evocative herbs and flowers.
- Needle and thread.
- Essential oils of your choice, we suggest lavender, rosemary and rose (optional).
- Colored sharpies or other pens, paints or embroidery thread (optional).
- Small pieces of paper to write spells, rune and sigils upon and place in the pillow.

Our favorite fresh dried flowers and herbs for dream pillows are lavender and mugwort. We also like to use chamomile, rosemary and a touch of cloves (three or four whole cloves per pillow will do!). Sometimes we add dried rose petals and hops. All of these are good for restful sleep and dreaming, and mugwort is particularly helpful for lucid dreaming. Mugwort (Artemisia vulgaris) is fairly easy to forage as it grows widespread in North America, Europe and Central and East Asia, but if you need to buy it you can find it in abundance for sale on the Internet.

Devil's Claw (Harpagophytum procumbens) root is used by many as a tea to enhance deep, lucid, dreaming. Some people call it the unicorn plant for its hornlike fruit. We like to use Devil's Claw root in our dream pillows, just be sure it is dried and ground well. You may buy it at a magick shop, but we actually began using it in our dream pillows in the 80s when Zardoa worked in Northern California at a nursery plant farm that also happened to have

Devil's Claw growing wild and in abundance. We found the dried hornlike fruit to make exotic decorations on the ends of wands (see Chapter 23 for a photo of our Devil's Claw wand) and the shavings from the roots to be perfect for putting inside our lucid dreaming pillows.

## Directions:

You could use an old pillowcase, but dream pillows are usually not very large. Still, there are small pillows one could use, take out the stuffing and fill it with the chosen herb. As we said Mugwort and Lavender are highly recommended.

If you have a bit of material, cut from an old pillowcase, or cut to size, of regular fabric, satin, or even soft upholstery fabric, you can easily make your own pillow. You may wish to make one end so it can be opened now and again to put in fresh herbs because the herbs will grow stale over time, although crushing the herbs while they are inside the pillow sometimes serves to refresh them. Mostly the evocative aspect of the pillow, besides the spell that is put upon it, is the fragrance you will be smelling when you are sleeping, which will then be arousing and triggering your subconscious and unconscious mind.

You may have to buy the herbs from an herb shop or on the Internet, especially if you live in the city. But these elves were fortunate to live near the woods when we were first into making dream pillows and we found mugwort, especially, and also lavender growing wild and in abundance near our house, so we'd just go out and collect some.

Stuff your pillow loosely with all herbs and flowers you wish to put in it. We like to use mostly mugwort, but add small amounts of the other herbs mentioned as well. Stuff it so it is almost full but soft to the touch. Also, if you can not find all the herbs and flowers that you wish to put in it, you can use drops of essential oils on satin stuffing or cotton batting. And of course, you can use any combination of herbs, flowers, silk strips or cotton batting, and essential oils. We prefer pillows with all fresh herbs and flowers but sometimes we freshen up our pillows by opening them up and adding a few drops of essential oils.

To make a pillow that will open easily, leave a flap of material, fold it over, stuff it and give it a loose stitch across. Or you could use Velcro of whatever you happen to think of. Snaps, or possibly even buttons might work, but you don't want anything that will disturb you when you sleep, like the rocks Samwise Gamgee always seemed to find in the *Lord of the Rings* when he and Frodo were living rough.

You may wish to decorate your dream pillow in some way. Embroider or paint on a spirit sigil or something else that will remind you of what you wish to invoke in your dreams. Perhaps, the sigil of a dream companion, protector or dream guide. You can also mark the pillow with a sharpie or other type of pen to do this. Of course, if you used upholstery material for your pillow, it may already have a design on it. In which case, you may wish to inscribe the spirit glyph or spell on a piece of paper that you put inside the pillow with the herbs you are using.

## Elven Spell Casting:

**CASTING A SPELL OF TRANSFORMATION:** (Use to help you or someone else to transform toward a better, more successful version of their s'elf.)
**"Deep within my (or your, if you are doing it for someone else) life is changed**
**Toward the better it's rearranged."**

(Arvyndase)
**"Dorae enåver el'na (le'na) ela da dylsïn**
**Lovur tae rilfa ter'da lopatunïn."**

(Pronunciation)
Door - ray e - nah - veer eel'nah (lee'nah) e - lah dah dills - in
Low - viewer tay rile - fah tier'dah low - pay - tune – in.


**SPELL FOR CALLING A DREAM GUARDIAN:**
**"As we through dreams do venture far**
**You'll ever know just where we are**
**And where we're going certain, sure**
**Clear the way forevermore."**

(Arvyndase)
**"Tat eli joul lovli ba halfan uli**
**Le'yon vari ken oda ern eli da**
**Nar ern eli'da tasdas imsa, vem**
**Vyrn tae yer varigostu."**

(Pronunciation)
Tate e - lie joe - yule low-v - lie bah hail - fane you - lie
Lee'yone vay - rye keen oh - dah ear-n e - lie dah
Nair ear-n e - lie'dah tace - dace I'm - sah, veem
Vern tay year vay - rye - go-ss – two.

**PROTECTOR SPELL:** (especially if you are lucid dreaming)
**"Ever safe in dreams I fly**
**To Astral Worlds both low and high."**

(Arvyndase)
**"Vari del ver lovli El fos**
**Va Basna Telthli aso dwa nar alt."**

The Silver Elves

(Pronunciation)
Vay - rye deal veer low-v - lie eel foe-ss
Vah Base - nah teal-th - lie dwah nair ale-t.


**FOR CALLING A PARTICULAR SPIRIT:**
**"Spirit (or the spirit's name) come and to me speak**
**As a better future we do seek."**

(Arvyndase)
**"Tari koso nar va el nor**
**Tat na rilfa lasel eli ba hed."**

(Pronunciation)
Tay - rye co - so nair vah eel nor
Tate nah rile - fah lay - seal e - lie bah heed.

**FORETELLING SPELL:** (for foreseeing the future)
**"All that comes to me is seen**
**Made most clear within my dream."**

(Arvyndase)
**"Wyl dij kosolu va el da tenïn**
**Kordïn erst vyrn enåver el'na lov."**

(Pronunciation)
Will dye-j co - so - lou vah eel dah teen - in
Cord - in ear-st vern e - nah - veer eel'nah low-v.


**LUCID DREAMING SPELL:** (to enhance lucid dreaming)
**"I awake within my dreams and steady I proceed**
**Waking only when I will or there is truly need."**

(Arvyndase)
**"El vasa enåver el'na lovli nar virba El murfan**
**Sildas norae nas El yon sa norn da lodla golt."**

(Pronunciation)
Eel vay - sah e - nah - veer eel'nah low-v – lie nair vie-r - bah Eel muir - fane
Sigh-l - dace nor - ray nace Eel yone sah nor-n dah load - lah goal-t.

# Chapter 8 . . . . Spell Crafting with a Seven Pointed Star

$\mathcal{E}$very time one draws a seven-pointed star, the star of the elves, a spell is cast to protect the elves and to help awaken our elven people. The fairies say: "If you believe in fairies, clap your hands." And with this act of clapping, the fairies are blessed. Elves say, "If you wish to give Elven blessings, draw a seven-pointed star" and with this magical act, a spell of opening the veil to Elfland manifesting on Earth is cast.

Many people refer to this as the Faery Star, however, it was first used as an elven symbol by the Elf Queen's Daughters in the mid 1970's when they/we (we were part of the Sisterhood of the Elf Queen's Daughters and had a vortex in Southern Illinois) were publishing *the Elf Magic Mail* (see our two volumes that have the text of these letters, discription of them and commentary upon them. Also, see our books *Magic Talks, Sorcerers' Dialogues, Discourses on High Sorcery* and *Ruminations on Necromancy*, which reproduce a correspondence between us and two of our sisters, who were the founders of the Elf Queen's Daughters).

We consider drawing an acute seven-pointed star to be one of our most important artistic skills, and it requires much practice to do it perfectly. We also consider the practice of drawing a seven-pointed star to be a meditation and to bring good luck and health to the artist. With the simple instructions below, you can learn to draw one without a protractor and without ever taking your pen up from the paper. All you need is paper and pen and time to practice.

**The Magical Image**: *The young elf masters the drawing of the septagram and uses hir skill to paint elf stars upon hir Elfin Book of Shadows.*

## Directions:

Remember to make this drawing without ever taking your pen off the paper! Even if they are not drawn perfectly, it just takes practice and each star that is drawn, perfect or not, will carry your magical intent. This is not really about making a perfect star but about becoming comfortable with the stars you make and yet improving your skill at making them at the same time. Also, if you wish to use a ruler, that's okay, too, but at least give this a try.

Here is a picture to help you easily learn to draw the seven-pointed star. First of all, note that the numbers in the circles are indicating drawing steps not the number of the ray points themselves. Just follow the numbers beginning with the #1 and trace the lines going to each next numbered step (returning to #1 after #7) with your fingers before trying to draw it on your paper. Although we do not show it in this diagram, the ray points are simply numbered beginning with the top point being the 1st Ray point and going clockwise, each point is numbered subsequently.

Remember that while drawing this star, you never need to pick your pen up from the paper. Here is another way of doing the same thing as tracing the numbers above:

- Imagine that the first ray point is at the top of the star, and there are seven ray points sequentially going clock-wise. First draw an upside down V. Do this by starting at the lower left side of where the drawing will be placed on the paper, draw up to the top point and then bring your pen down to the right, so a symmetrical upside down V is drawn. This makes the points drawn starting at the 5th to the 1st and then to the 4th rays. **Do not lift your pen from the paper.**

- Continue by drawing a straight line at an upward angle to the left about 2/3(+ a little) of the way up crossing over the upside down V and this will make the point for the 7th ray.

- Draw a straight horizontal line at a downward angle to the right crossing back over the upside down V and ending at the right side, a little more than half of the way down. This makes the point for the 3rd ray.

- Now draw straight across, horizontally to the left, to a point a little more than half the way down on that side, to make a ray point that is symmetrical to the point in step 3. This makes the 6th ray point.

- Draw back to the top on the right side of the star to match in symmetry to the 7th ray point on the left that you drew in step 2. This makes the ray point for the 2nd ray.

- Finish drawing your acute seven-pointed star by drawing a line that connects it back to where you started. You will both begin and end on the point of the 5th ray. Remember, the whole time you are really just drawing symmetrical V's. Also, if you wish to draw regular V's and then turn the star around or have a downward pointing Elf Star, that's okay as well. Magically, we use the downward pointing Elf Star for invoking forces into the world, bringing the light of Elfin down upon the material plane and use the upward pointing star for our aspirations toward the higher realms of spirit, the realms of the Shining Ones.

Also, if you have a graphics program such as Illustrator, it is really easy to create perfectly symmetrical Elf Stars. Still, sometimes you may wish to do it by hand for some quick magic and elven blessings when you are about in the world.

Years ago, these elves knew a witch who would hang out with us sometimes who asked us to go with her when she visited a house in the country to look at a room that she was considering renting. She had just divorced and needed to move out of her husband's place. As we examined the new place, she noticed a small upside down five pointed star, which is often used by the media to represent Satanism, drawn on the back of the front door, and she freaked out.

We elves laughed. First, we don't have a kneejerk reaction to Satanism as some folks have and we take what the media says with only a bit more than a grain of salt (for protection). And it was clear to us and we pointed out to her that considering its height on the door it was probably drawn by a small child, which in fact turned out to be the case. It seemed upside down because the child, as they tend to do, tilted hir (his or her) hand when drawing it.

But this brings us to the point that unlike the pentagram, which is sometimes genuinely and often erroneously associated with Satanism, especially when it is pointing downward, the Elf Star has no negative connotations whether it is upward, downward or sideways. The difference, as we say, is merely one of purpose and while we don't usually have our Elf Stars pointing sideways, we expect that if you did so you could use it to indicate new and perhaps surprising directions in your life.

## Meditations on the Seven-Pointed Elven Star

The following is an excerpt from the meditation on the seven-pointed elven star that originally appeared in the 1986 Summer edition of *Circle Network News,* in an article "Elven Group Dynamics and Bonding Ritual" written by the Silver Elves. This was a meditation that Silver Flame created and performed for Zardoa's 39th birthday gift. She meditated on each ray point of the seven-pointed elven star, one day at a time, leading up to his birthday. Later the following year, Zardoa asked her to submit this meditation to *Circle* as a part of the article they wrote. Since the time it appeared in *Circle,* many people have revised this original meditation to transform it using their own ideas and cosmology, but the idea of the mediation opening the Gateway to Elfin [Faerie Realms] has remained, as well as the healing aspect and outcome of love and magic for Mother Earth [Gaia Consciousness].

### "Meditations on the Seven Pointed Star"

**Point 1:** Meditate on **The Sun**, our nearest star, the **Gate to bring Peace and Prosperity in Elfland**. The Dragon of Truth, Love & Justice is linked to this point.

**Point 2:** Meditate upon **The Spirits of the Trees**. **Loving Friendship** and healing light [unconditional love].

**Point 3**: Meditate upon Regenerative Powers and **Creative Energy**. **Spirit of the Waters** cleanses, bringing with it an Awakening of your True Nature.

**Point 4:** Meditate upon the Gift of **Magic** and Elven Blessings. **"Love is Magic, Magic is Love."**

**Point 5:** Meditate upon **The Gateway,** on having Prosperity and Peace needed for an Entry into Elfland, **[Passage into Faerie]**.

**Point 6:** Meditate upon **Justice** in the Faerie Realms, **Healing** [of the Elfae]. **Wind Spirits.**

**Point 7:** Meditate upon success in "Extending your **Love and Magic to All Life;** to Mother Earth **[Gaia Consciousness].**"

We suggest that you make an offering to the spirits each of the seven days of your meditation and there is no better gift than the gift of art making. We have performed this meditation many times since we first created it in the 80s and like to paint and meditate upon a magic elf rock on each of the seven days, painting on the rock an elven rune or sigil of an elven spirit from our book *The Elfin Book of Spirits* (see Chapter 15 for more on magic elf rocks).

We Silver Elves love the Elven Star. We always have, from the first time our sisters of the Elf Queen's Daughter put it on their letters in the mid 70s, it sang to our hearts as it clearly sings to the hearts of thousands of fae folk. We wear it as an amulet and have done so for over 40 years. We sometimes wear it on our hats. We have at least ten versions of it on the walls of our bedroom and a number in our living room and kitchen. If it sings to your heart as well, let it bless your life as it has ours and spread those blessings into the world touching all and making the world a more magical, beautiful and wondrous place to be.

## Elven Spell Casting

**POINT ONE SPELL:**
**"All I will shall manifest**
**Tried and true and pass the test."**

(Arvyndase)
**"Wyl El yon van aroto**
**Ujïn nar lod nar gol tae fatra."**

(Pronunciation)
Will Eel yone vane a - row - toe
You-j - in nair load nair goal tay fay – trah.

**POINT TWO SPELL:**
**"Elf friends true shall with me be**
**We shall be bound in loyalty."**

(Arvyndase)
**"Êlda edarli lod van ena el te**
**Eli van te cyrnïn ver tutåtu."**

(Pronunciation)
L - dah e - dare - lie load vane e - nah eel tea
E - lie vane tea sern - in veer two - tah — two.


**POINT THREE SPELL:**
"**Bright and new we make the way**
**Born again on every day.**"

(Arvyndase)
"**Ilu nar fae eli kord tae yer**
**Daend sasnana ton lotym lea.**"

(Pronunciation)
Eye - lou nair fay e - lie cord tay year
Day - eend sayce - nay - nah tone low - tim lee — ah.


**POINT FOUR SPELL:**
"**Elfin blessings among us shared**
**Among those who loved and those who cared.**"

(Arvyndase)
"**Êldat elsordas arae eli matiïn**
**Arae dijli jae kyêlåïn nar dijli jae synthïn.**"

(Pronunciation)
L - date eel - soar - dace a - ray e - lie may - tie - in
A - ray dye-j - lie jay key - l - lah - in nair dye-j - lie jay sinth — in.


**POINT FIVE SPELL:**
"**Faerie rises all about**
**With song and dance and joyous shout.**"

(Arvyndase)
"**Farri luftlu wyl basar**
**Ena lora nar far nair elsåsey ontar.**"

(Pronunciation)
Fay - rye lew-ft - lou will bay - sair
E - nah low - rah nair fair nair eel - sah - say ohn — tayr.

**POINT SIX SPELL:**
"Justice in Faerie for one and for all
Together we rise, we let none of us fall."

(Arvyndase)
**Eldan eli luft,  eli lao konar u eli lot."
"Vafar ver Farri fro ata nar fro wyl**

(Pronunciation)
Vay - fair veer Fair - rye fro a - tah nair fro will
Eel - dane e - lie lew-ft, e - lie lay - oh co - nair you e - lie lote.

**POINT SEVEN SPELL:**
"Ever we share our magic and love
Creating the Earth as Elfin above."

(Arvyndase)
**"Vari eli mati eli'na êldon nar kyêla
Talysdas tae Eldanil tat Êldat usel."**

(Pronunciation)
Vay - rye e - lie may - tie e - lie'nah l - doan nair key - l - lah
Tay - liss - dace tay Eel - day - nile tate L - date you – seal.

**ELVEN STAR SPELL:** (Use as an overall spell with the elf star as a focus.)
**"By the Elf Star the Earth is healed
And to our magic all do yield."**

(Arvyndase)
**"La tae Êlda Mêl tae Eldanil da hyrnïn
Nar va eli'na êldon wyl ba ped."**

(Pronunciation)
Lah  tay L - dah Mell tay Eel - day - nile dah herne - in
Nair vah e - lie'nah l - doan will bah peed.

"May the light of the elven stars shine in your heart and guide you wherever you go."
—Elven farewell.

# Chapter 9 . . . . Elven Mbuti

We elves enjoy making Mbuti art, as it touches into our most ancient elven art traditions. This is art for the more wild elves to release our primal elven spirit. It is an art of the wee people or the Ituri forest people of Africa and is still practiced today by some tribes in the African Rainforest. The Mbuti use painted cloths made of the bark of six species of trees from the rainforest, and it is prepared by the men and then painted by the women. This cloth is used as ritual dress for festivals, celebrations and rites of passage and initiations, as well as for wedding and funeral ceremonies. We, of course, do not have access to this bark, so instead we use brown paper that we treat to have a similar look and will share this process with you in this chapter.

Traditionally, the Mbuti artists use a variety of biomorphic motifs like butterflies, birds, and leopard spots and also geometric patterns that give an impression of sound, motion, and shapes that are found within the rainforest. You may see motifs resembling the light that is filtered through the trees, or the buzzing of insects, ant trails, or of vines. And they use crosshatched squares to represent the texture of reptilian skin, turtles, crocodiles or snakes. The example of the two Mbuti cloths at the beginning of this chapter are the first ones that we made and we used stars and spirals of our own elven traditions as our main motifs, although we were trying to stay somewhat within the tradition of the Mbuti or Bamiki Bandura people, "the children of the forest."

We were first introduced to this art form in an art class at our local community college, which, as it happened, was rated as the second best community college in the nation. We took classes in painting, drawing, color mixing and other art processes. Of all the art processes that we learned, Mbuti art was one of our favorites and we truly think you would love it too. It is a lot of fun and has a little bit of the feeling of banner making attached to it. Creating Mbuti art will take your soul and imagination back into the ancient forest, even if you are a modern city dwelling elf!

**The Magical Image:** *The elven artist magically draws into hir world the life and breath of the planet.*

## Materials Needed:

- You will need Acrylic or other paints and small fine brushes. Paints need to be a variety of earth, sun and sky colors, including greens, browns, gray, blues, with some orange and maroons. There are really no limits; you will be using colors to paint motifs that represent the forest, ocean, sun, stars, as well as symbols of your magic.
- Also, you will need a large paper bag from a grocery store or brown wrapping paper to cut a piece approximately 36 by 18 inches, although it is meant to be an unusual and uneven shape, as you can see in the photo in the beginning of this chapter, almost like you were painting it on an animal pelt.

## Directions:

The first thing to do is to prepare the paper. You need to tear the edges of your piece into the shape you will be using. As we have pointed out, this is meant to be an odd shape and approximately 36 by 18 inches. Next wad up the paper, try not to tear it. (But if you do tear it, don't worry, as it will just give it an interesting authentic look.) Then straighten it out again and soak it in a pan of water for 5 minutes until completely wet. Now remove it from the water to allow it to dry on a flat surface. Once it is dry, it should be crinkly looking, giving it the appearance of bark cloth.

If you don't have old-fashioned paper bags available, you can get large pieces of paper and dye them with old coffee or tea grounds boiled in water. After it cools, pour the water with grounds over the paper to dye it and let it dry. After the paper dries, shake off any grounds left on it. If you can't find large enough pieces, you can use string to stitch together a number of pieces. This can look pretty interesting, really.

On a blank piece of drawing paper, begin by doodling a number of simple motifs that relate to your elements or elementals, your allies, kin type, spirits and to your magic. Keep these very simple, as they will be repeated symbols painted on your paper. We elven like to use stars (try the seven pointed elven star) in our Mbuti, as well as spirals, outlines of leaves, totem animal tracks, feathers, flowers, trees, the moon, the sun and other aspects of nature, as well as our elven magical rune symbols and spirit sigils and other glyphs, such as astrological, alchemical and planetary symbols. And remember that blank areas between the patterns are also very important. In the rainforest the quiet means peace and lack of noise and conflict.

Once you have a variety of images to use and your paper is completely dry, you may begin by randomly dividing the paper up using white or black as an outline of various sections in which you will paint your motifs. Next, begin painting repeated symbols in the different sections. This is the tedious part and we suggest you play some beautiful elven music and enjoy the process as a meditation.

## Elven Spell Casting:

The spells that enchant your Mbuti paintings can be of a great variety, but also remember they usually involve the Universe, the Earth, the forests and Elfin and Faerie, also.

**ELEMENTAL SPELL:** (Use for summoning a particular elemental through the magic of your Mbuti. Remember, you can use more than one spell.)

**EARTH:**
**"Established now our elfin band**
**Secure within this elvish land."**

(Arvyndase)
**"Norsetyrïn mat eli'na êldat dårn**
**Yader enåver wyr êldåtu taru."**

(Pronunciation)
Nor - see - ter - in mate e - lie'nah l - date darn
Yeah - deer e - nah - veer were l - dah - two tay – rue.

**FIRE:**
**"Energized and spirit charged**
**Our elfin powers now enlarged."**

(Arvyndase)
**"Didaronåïn nar tari fylreïn**
**Eli'na êldat eldroli mat tahilvarïn."**

(Pronunciation)
Dye - dare - row - nah - in nair tay - rye fill - ree – in
E - lie'nah l - date eel - drow - lie mate tay - hiel - vayr – in.

## AIR:
**"The power of the air we find**
**Awakes now in our elven mind."**

(Arvyndase)
**"Tae eldro u tae eron eli låc**
**Vasålu mat ver eli'na êldata car."**

(Pronunciation)
Tay - eel - drow you tay e - roan e - lie lock
Vay - sah - lou mate veer e - lie'nah l - day - tah car.

## WATER:
**"One together, one apart**
**One forever from the start."**

(Arvyndase)
**"Ata eldan, ata eperat**
**Ata varigos an tae altu."**

(Pronunciation)
A - tah eel - dane, a - tah e - peer - rate
A - tah vay - rye - go-ss ane tay ale – two.

## SPIRIT:
**"Ever upward we aspire**
**Ever climbing, ever higher."**

(Arvyndase)
**"Vari repvur eli watan**
**Vari lypyndas, vari altfa."**

(Pronunciation)
Vay - rye reap - viewer e - lie way - tane
Vay - rye lip - pen - dace, vay - rye ale-t – fah.

Or the Asian elemental system

EARTH:
**"Arising now upon the Earth
To Elfin true we now give birth."**

(Arvyndase)
**"Valufodas mat repton tae Eldanil
Va Êldat lod eli mat luth daen."**

(Pronunciation)
Vay - lou - foe - dace mate reap - tone tay Eel - day - nile
Vah L - date load e - lie mate lew-th day – een.


FIRE:
**"Filled with life and fiery power
A blessing upon this elven bower."**

(Arvyndase)
**"Ulåïn ena ela nar furnath eldro
Na elsordas repton wyr êldata dysor."**

(Pronunciation)
You - lah - in e - nah e - lah nair few-r - nayth eel - drow
Nah eel - soar - dace reap - tone were l - day - tah diss – soar.


WATER:
**"Fluid like water we flow and bond
Joyous together, forever fond."**

(Arvyndase)
**"Folse sylar quant eli sur nar ellani
Elsåsey eldan, varigos fore."**

(Pronunciation)
Foal - see sill - lair que - ain't e - lie sewer nair eel - lane - nigh
Eel - sah - say eel - dane, vay - rye - go-ss for – ree.

**WOOD:**
"Beneath the trees we sway with the wind
The breath of new knowledge ever our friend."

(Arvyndase)
"Usco tae aldåli eli yof ena tae solon
Tae shol u fae kenvu vari eli'na edar."

(Pronunciation)
Youse - co tay ale - dah -lie e - lie yoe-f e - nah tay so - lone
Tay shoal you fay keen - view vay - rye e - lie'nah e – dare.

**METAL:**
"Hard as metal, strong as steel
Power used for the commonweal. "

(Arvyndase)
"Tarl tat rarok, mylth tat ruko
Eldro nosïn fro tae byraldolj."

(Pronunciation)
Tayr-l tate ray - roke, mill-th tate rue - co
Eel - drow noss - in fro tay ber - rail - dole-j.

**ELFIN BLESSING SPELL:**
"Elfin blessings upon this home
With us here and wherever we roam."

(Arvyndase)
"Êldat elsordasli repton wyr elum
Ena eli jän nar ernvari eli dune."

(Pronunciation)
L - date eel - soar - dace - lie reap - tone were e - loom
E - nah - e - lie jan nair ear-n - vay - rye e - lie due – knee.

**EVOCATION OF FAERIE SPELL:**
"Faerie manifest all around
From the sky down to the ground."

(Arvyndase)
**"Farri aroto wyl anabo
An tae faln dab va tae durm."**

(Pronunciation)
"Fay - rye a - row - toe will a - nay -bow
Ane tay fail-n day-b vah tay due-rm."


**ELVISH REALM SPELL:**
**"Elfin emerges, comes to life
Awakened, harmonious without strife."**

(Arvyndase)
**"Êldat amlu, kosolu va ela
Vasåtåïn, belosey enåkon scurv."**

(Pronunciation)
L - date aim - lu, co - so - lou vah e - lah
Vay - sah - tah - in, be - low - say e - nah - cone scurve.


**SPIRIT BLESSINGS SPELL:**
**"Greatly bless this realm of ours
Here on Earth and among the stars."**

(Arvyndase)
**"Raltla elsor wyr êld u eli'na
Jän ton Eldanil nar arae tae mêlli."**

(Pronunciation)
Rail-t - lah eel - soar were eald you e - lie'nah
Jan tone Eel - day - nile nair air - ray tay mell – lie.

**"Make your magic such that other people are glad they are alive to see and experience it."** —Elven Admonition.


**"Elves leave enchantment everywhere the way other people leave fingerprints."**

# Chapter 10 . . . . Faerie Dust, Pixie Powder, and Prosperity Powder

These elves have long enjoyed making batches of Faerie Dust or what we have also called Pixie Powder and Prosperity Powder. We use Pixie Powder or Prosperity Powder in our magic circles for enchanting helpful spirits to come to us, to enliven parties by sprinkling it on the dance floor, and for bringing prosperity to our eald by sprinkling it around all floor areas after we clean the house, in our mailboxes, in our purses, on ourselves for empowerment, and anywhere else that we want prosperity to increase. Pixie Powder, Elf Dust, Faerie Elf Light, Elf Luster, is also known as Shimmering and is an ancient elfin means of increasing the magic of all occasions and places.

**Blow pixie powder wherever needed, or sprinkle it about to increase your luck and wellbeing and bring you closer to the devanic spirits of nature called elves, faeries, sprites, gnomes, brownies, undines, nymphs, dryads, sylphs, satyrs, leprechauns, etc....**

For several years in the late 70s and 80s, we Silver Elves made our own Prosperity Powder and used it in our magic circles with groups of elves to evoke elven spirits that would both benefit the members of the circle and all elven folk in general. Then later, in the 90s, we made our own Pixie Powder (and sometimes called it Faerie Dust) and enjoyed gifting it to our elven brothers and sisters, as well as selling it for a $1 a bag in our booth at the local market. On the previous page is a photo of the pamphlet and original artwork to which we attached the bag of Pixie Powder. The art was drawn by our late elven-ranger brother Danyêl, who appeared with us in the photo accompanying an article about Faery Folk in *Renaissance Magazine* #15. Danyêl was an accomplished artist, and he drew the picture for the little card that explained Pixie Powder, and its uses in drawing luck to one's s'elf and in drawing our kindred to us.

If you do make your own and you sell it or gift it to others, be sure to add a reminder note on your batch that says, "Not for internal consumption!" (unless of course you use all eatable flowers).

**The Magical Image:** *Upon two lovers, the woodland elf sprinkles Shimmer, made of flowers elven picked and elven thrice blessed to increase luck and prosperity.*

## Materials Needed:

You will want to collect flowers that have fallen to the ground (we are elven hedgewitches, after all). Roses, hydrangea, lavender, sea holly, celosia, yarrow, strawflower, globe amaranth, bachelor's buttons work well and if you live in a tropical climate then you are in luck if you have a plumeria flowering tree near you for it will have new flowers falling every morning. Just be certain that you use flowers that are not poisonous in any way. You will also need a flat pan to lay them on during the drying process. Place them in an area in the house that will be undisturbed and dry. We have always used the top of the refrigerator. Once dry, crushed and ground, place your flower dust, pixie power in a wooden or ceramic bowl and use in liberal amounts.

## Directions:

The process of making this magical powder is very simple. Collect flowers that have fallen to the ground and put them out on a flat surface to dry. Once all the flowers are dry, crumble them up and put them in a blender or coffee grinder (or hand grind with the use of a mortar and pestle) to process and make a fine powder out of them. It is that simple to make!

Some elves and especially faeries like to add glitter to the mix; it gives it that sparkly look. We prefer very fine glitter over the larger pieces. Also, you can add cinnamon, or ginger or some other spices, but spices can be expensive so we mostly do without them. Yet, sometimes you can find old spices that are past their use by date on your own shelf or that someone has discard that while no longer suited for consumption may work perfectly well in prosperity powder. Waste not, want not! We elves love to take what others have thrown away and turn it into art and/or magic.

Use as needed or as it suits your fancy. Spread it about as you cast elven spells and it will soon attract the elfin spirits eager to be of service to those who still believe in them.

## Elven Spell Casting

**PROSPERITY SPELL:** (for general prosperity and success)
**"Success comes now, success comes here**
**Banishes all worries and all fear."**

(Arvyndase)
**"Reda kosolu mat, reda kosolu jän**
**Grynkaslu wyl vorgili nar wyl mak."**

(Pronunciation)
Re - dah co - so - lou mate, re - dah co - so - lou jan
Grin - case - lou will vour - guy - lie nair will make

**ATTRACTION SPELL: (**for attracting one's elf friends and kindred)
**"Like magnets we attract our kin**
**Lovers true and elven friend."**

(Arvyndase)
**"Sylar rakali eli chanae eli'na eldi**
**Kyêlåfåli lod nar êldata edar."**

(Pronunciation)
Sill - lair ray - kay - lie e - lie chay - nae e - lie'nah eel - die
Key - l - lah - fah - lie load nair l - day - tah e - dare

**MONEY DRAWING SPELL:** (specifically for increasing wealth)
**"Swiftly dollars (or Euros, Pounds, Yen, etc.) come to me**
**Creating wealth repeatedly**
**Always when the need is great**
**Abundantly and never late."**

(Arvyndase)
**"Vysla pamali koso va el**
**Talysdas doljver daranla**
**Verat nas tae zanti da ralt**
**Konåkorla nar konzar vin."**

(Pronunciation)

Viss - lah pay - may - lie co - so vah eel

Tay - liss - dace dole-j - veer dare - rain - lah

Veer - rate nace tay zane - tie dah rail-t

Cone - nah - core - lah nair cone - zair vine.

**S'ELF HEALING SPELL:**
**"Body, mind, spirit and soul**
**In every way, I am made whole."**

(Arvyndase)
**"Miwa, car, tari nar der**
**Ver lotym yer, El da kordïn loj."**

(Pronunciation)

Me - wah, car, tay - rye nair deer

Veer low - tim year, Eel dah cord - in low-j.

**OTHER HEALING SPELL:** (for healing others)
**"From every ill you are now healed**
**To our bright magics you do yield."**

(Arvyndase)
**"An lotym nål le da mat hyrnïn**
**Va eli'na ilu êldonli le ba ped."**

(Pronunciation)

Ane low - tim nahl lee dah mate herne - in

Vah e - lie'nah eye - lou l - doan - lie lee bah peed.

**AMBIENCE SPELL:** (Use for creating a positive and magical ambience or atmosphere for your home or some other place.)
**"Within our eald magic sings**
**And greater magic still it brings**
**Joy and kinship we do share**
**With happiness and loving care."**

(Arvyndase)
**"Enåver eli'na ald êldon fondlu**
**Nar raltfa êldon vila ter curalu**
**Elsa nar elditu eli ba mati**
**Ena ejartu nar kyêlådas synth."**

(Pronunciation)
E - nah - veer e - lie'nah ale-d l - doan phoned - lu
Nair  rail-t - fah l - doan vie - lah tier cur - rah - lu
Eel - sah nair eel - dye - two e - lie bah may - tie
E - nah e - jayr - two nair key - l - lah - dace synth.


**AWAKENING SPELL:** (to heal those who are awakening to their true elfin nature)
**"Stirring in your heart and mind**
**The seed of your true s'elf you find**
**Awakening now, embracing strong**
**The s'elf within for whom you long."**


(Arvyndase)
**"Charlos ver le'na bom nar car**
**Tae dern u le'na lod eln le låc**
**Vasådas mat, byrhådas mylth**
**Tae eln enåver fro jae le awath."**


(Pronunciation)
Char - lowce veer lee'nah bowm nair car
Tay deer-n you lee'nah load eel-n lee lock
Vay - sah - dace mate, ber - hah - dace mill-th
Tay eel-n e - nah - veer fro jay lee a – wayth.


**ELVEN BLESSING SPELL:**
**"Better now your life becomes**
**About you magic swirls and hums."**


(Arvyndase)
**"Rilfa mat le'na ela casalu**
**Basar le êldon mushlu nar zermlu."**


(Pronunciation)
Rile-fa mate lee'nah e - lah cah - say - lou
Bay - sayr lee l - doan mew-sh - lou nair zeerm – lou.


**JOB HUNTING SPELL:** (Use for getting a particular job as long as it is in harmony with your greater Destiny.)
**"The job I wish for shall be mine**
**If Destiny does itself incline."**

(Arvyndase)
**"Tae farm El felj fro van te el'na**
**Nef Lawath ba terelde tolen."**

(Pronunciation)
Tay fair-m Eel feel-j fro vane tea eel'nah
Neef Lay - wayth bah tier - eel - dee toe – lean.

**ENLIGHTENMENT SPELL:** (Use for increasing your wisdom, knowledge and understanding in all ways.)
**"Great the light that in me blooms**
**In the dark revelation looms."**

(Arvyndase)
**"Ralt tae lun dij ver el flulu**
**Ver tae das lifardur almolu."**

(Pronunciation)
Rail-t tay loon dye-j veer eel flew - lou
Veer tay dace lie - fair - dure ale - moe – lou.

**"Pixie powder and faerie dust, we give what we can, you take what you must."**

**"Every gift an elf gives has magic at its core."**
**—Old Elven Saying**

**"When you are touched by magic, everything seems magical."**
**—Elven Observation.**

**"In economics, there's a principle of supply and demand. In elvish magic, there's a principle of supply on demand. When you truly wish for something, it comes. Perhaps not right away. It all depends on the distance it must travel to get to you. But it comes."**
**—Ancient Elven Knowledge**

# Chapter 11 . . . . Making Fairy Houses and Elf Villages

Many awakened elfae will say that one of the very first signs that they had as a young child that they were fae is that they loved making fairy houses to commune with the faeries. Of course, one can begin making fairy houses and elf villages at any age and recapture the feeling of awe and wonder that is experienced when doing so. You can find numerous people on the Internet these days who have made an advocation and sometimes a profession of making Fairy Houses, many of them quite wonderful to behold.

## Fairy Houses

As a very young child, Silver Flame would talk to the fairies and then make them fairy houses out of old shoe boxes, putting cotton balls in little half-opened empty match boxes for beds in which the fairies could rest (she could be found scavenging the household trashcans daily to find all of her art supplies), setting thimbles up-side-down for tables, and leaving small pieces of bread on the thimble tables for them to dine upon. Now some decades later, she still enjoys making fairy houses, often putting them next to trees or near creek beds. She makes them from found objects in nature like rocks, sea shells, stems, tree bark, small branches, moss, flowers and leaves, along with occasional pieces of beautiful silk scarves or ribbons.

The fairy nest in the photo to the right is one she made out of mostly bark and feathers. She tucked inside a magical wish written on a small piece of paper, and left it for the fairies at the base of a grandfather oak tree in Sonoma County, California. It is in the making of these little fairy homes that we elves leave our magical blessings for the wild fairy spirits. And we have often, in turn, been given invitations to join them in the moonlight to dance in celebration of their newly found magical home.

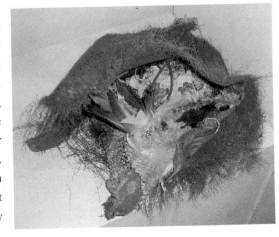

Of course, we also still love to make fairy and elven houses using beautiful cloth material, feathers, scraps of wood, boxes, and a variety of other discarded building materials. One of our favorite elven houses is for the Menehuni, the Hawaii elves (see photo below).

**The Magical Image***: The elven princess creates fairy homes to set among the trees, where later she dances under the moonlight in a fairy ring.*

Elven and Fairy houses: (Left) House for Menehune, wee folk, in Hawaii
(Middle bottom) Silk and glitter invisible fairy house, only
those kindred of faerie can see it well (Right) Elf Hall.

## Elven Spell Casting

**INVITATION SPELL:** (to invite the faeries to live within the fairy house you have created for them)
**"Fairy home, elven hall,**
**May you all come and have a ball!"**

(Arvyndase)
**"Farri elum, êldata alon,**
**Me le wyl koso nar tir na tarla!"**

(Pronunciation)
Fair - rye e - loom, l - day - tah a - lone,
Me lee will co - so nair tire nah tayr - lah!

**FAIRY HOME SPELL:**
**"Bright elven spirits abide here within**
**Spreading your magic with joy and a grin."**

(Arvyndase)
**"Ilu êldata tarili ruden jän enåver**
**Wyddas le'na êldon ena elsa nar na visol."**

(Pronunciation)
Eye - lou l - day - tah tayr - rye - lie rue - dean jan e - nah - veer
Wid - dace lee'nah l - doan e - nah eel - sah nair nah vie – soul.

**MIRROR SPELL:** (Use so that your elf home or fairy house will be like a voodoo doll, or in this case a voodoo dwelling reflecting your own home and spreading luck and blessings upon you, your family and the house and all who dwell there or come to visit.)
**"As below, so above**
**In peace and harmony and in love."**

(Arvyndase)
**"Tat yana, re usel**
**Ver qua nar belo nar ver kyêla."**

(Pronunciation)
Tate yeah - nah, ree you - seal
Veer que - ah nair be - low nair veer key - l – lah.

# Elf Villages

You may also enjoy making elven villages, allowing yourself to imagine a communal living space for yourself and other elves. There is a powerful magic embodying something in your imagination into physical form and we often use art as a magical step in the manifesting of our dreams, our goals and intentions. It is, in its way, a symbolic communication to the spirit world, letting the higher elfin spirits know what we desire.

**The Magical Image**: *A wizard manifests Elfland using the magic of art.*

Using bamboo, moss, palm bark, wood glue, Zardoa created a three-story elven tree-house village — an elven dream of communal life. He first built the basic structures of each floor, stacking them securely, and then added in the fun details like a long slide from the second floor to the garden area, furniture, a look-out tower, stairs and ladders. He used little figures he bought from the dollar store of punk rock figures and martial arts figures to use as elves and pixies, which he placed in the village. He painted them, and using Sculpey polymer clay created elf ears that he secured using thin wire for an ear shaped frame that he glued into holes drilled into the side of their heads (so the ears wouldn't just fall off), and also added bows and arrows and other elven paraphernalia.

(Left) Zardoa's Elf Village. You can see the look-out tower at the top in this three-story tree house community elf village, with rope stairs between floors and a long slide on the left to the garden area. (Right) A close-up of the second floor living space of the Elf Village with elves and pixies sleeping and others dancing about.

While these are small elf houses, castles and villages, somewhat like one might use in D&D gaming, we should note that boys, especially, have been building tree forts for ages on a larger scale and those are elf houses as well. Some elfin have even made real elf tree houses to live in, and that is really manifesting Elfin in a sense.

These elves were once visiting some elf kin who live in the mountains of Northern California whose two young boys eagerly showed us the small Elven Rath they had built. A circular construction of tree branches that blended into the forest around it but had small openings so that when you crawled inside you could see all around you from hiding. We might mention that Hunter's "hides" are really another form of this elven abode, although we elves never hunt for sport. The animals' lives, as well as the lives of the trees, are sacred to us.

We also like to build castles for our elven and faerie royalty. Zardoa built the castle pictured on the right using discarded corrugated cardboard and Styrofoam as a base, painting it to look like stones.

Not everyone has the wherewithal or resides in a place where creating an elven tree home is feasible. Many of us live in the city, often some distance from a forest or wooded area. And so we must remember that our art pieces are reflections of the true Realm of Elfin that we are manifesting and that even in an apartment, we can create our own magical ealds or elven homes. The creative activities described in this book are art processes used as magical tools. Elven home decor is also a magical and enchanting process, a type of spell casting on a larger scale. Make your home as elven, or faerie, as you can and bring Elfin and Faerie alive in your life and thus into the world.

## Elven Spell Casting

MANIFESTING ELFIN SPELL: (to use your elf village as a spell for attracting and manifesting an elven community)
**"From this seed a world is born
Arising on the bright elf morn."**

(Arvyndase)
**"An wyr dern na telth da daend
Valufodas ton tae ilu êlda calf."**

(Pronunciation)
Ane were deer-n nah teal-th dah day - eend
Vah - lou - foe - dace tone tay eye - lou l - dah cal-f.

HOME BLESSING SPELL:
**"All enchantments we now spell
Within our home do now dwell."**

(Arvyndase)
**"Wyl syrandirli eli mat moja
Enåver eli'na elum ba mat lefwa."**

(Pronunciation)
Will sir - rain - dire - lie e - lie mate moe - jah
E - nah - veer e - lie'nah e - loom bah mate leaf – wah.

**COMMUNITY SPELL:** (Use for gathering a group together and using your elf home structure as a energetic symbol to activate elven community.)
**"Ever growing larger till reality must agree**
**Elfin manifests here now in living community."**

(Arvyndase)
**"Vari lythdas hïlvfa ted althtu sarb ora**
**Êldat arotolu jän mat ver alsardas eldartu."**

(Pronunciation)
Vay - rye lith - dace hill-v - fah teed ale-th - two sayr-b or - rah
L - date a - row - toe - lou jan mate veer ale - sayr - dace eel - dare – two.

**"We heed the Call of Elfin true,**
**It's ever here for me and you.**
**We're ever one whereever we roam,**
**And whereever we are waits Elfin our home."**

**"Every choice shifts us into another dimension.**
**Thus, when we live our lives as elves we get closer and closer to Elfin manifest."**
**—Old Elven Saying**

**"Elfin's a world that's born of dreams,**
**Entwined upon their touching seams,**
**Creating a world that's greater still**
**Where every soul can love fulfill."**

# Chapter 12 . . . . Elven Group Art

When elves play games, everyone wins! When elves do art, it is also often done together as one united creative effort. We love to create together and we thus make our magic as one. So whether we are playing a game or doing art, we do it cooperatively. There is an old elven chant that we like to say as we create art together: "Together Our Magic is Stronger By Far!" And it is! This is, of course, the idea behind a coven for witches, or as we elves call it, a vortex, a swirling circle of elven creativity united and functioning as one.

## Notan: Awakening the Imagination

The Japanese art of Notan uses black-white contrast to demonstrate the concept of positive and negative space. It shows how the subject and the space around it are equally important. This is an art process we learned in a studio class while taking classes in fine arts at our local community college and one that is often taught to beginning art students. Our art teacher, John Watrous, extended the black and white version of making notan art to a more colorful version that we think you will enjoy doing as collaborative art with your tribe and as part of your magic. This particular process we are demonstrating is one that we used further in a number of Psychology of Creativity classes at Sonoma State University in which we had the pleasure of being intern teachers as graduate students. We always found people both enjoyed it and learned quite a bit about themselves and discovered quite a bit about those with whom they shared the experience. In fact, a number of people liked it so much that they began using it as a group icebreaker at personal parties.

**The Magical Image:** *The elf uses the art of notan as a zen meditation to learn balance.*

## Materials Needed:

- Black construction paper about 18 inches by 24 inches (can be smaller if necessary), one for each pair of participants
- Pack of variety of colors of construction paper, 8 ½ by 11 inches
- Scissors and paste for each person

## Directions:

Find an art partner. Two people work well for the first time, but after you get the hang of it, you can try four people. We suggest you keep it an even number. Sit together, and have each person cut out of colored construction paper pairs of random shapes. You may fold the paper or use two pieces together to create symmetrical designs. Cut for about 20 minutes. You may have a theme or you may just see what emerges from your collective unconscious. Now take a large piece of black construction paper (or a dark solid color you did not use in cutting the designs) and use that as the backdrop canvas for the art. Place the paper/canvas on a table. Choose together (giving each person a turn one at a time) which pieces to use (selecting from the pieces each has cut) and where to place them on the canvas/paper. You may place the pieces in symmetry or not, that is completely up to the artists. Glue the pieces on after they are all placed. You may leave it as it is or embellish it with whatever you like, colored pencils, glitter, sequins, feathers, etc. Just let your imaginations go wild!

Using the directions just given, pictured on the right is an example of a notan that Zardoa and Silver Flame created together and hung up in their eald in California for many years. In the color version of this notan image, you would see that the shapes are actually in orange, yellow, purple, brown, white, and pink.

Note that there is a certain spirit feel to it, like one is creating glyphs for calling the spirits and surely one is if one adds one's spells and intentions to the art process.

## Elven Spell Casting:

**SPIRIT SUMMONING SPELL**: (Use for summoning a particular spirit into your dwelling or a particular area where you decide to hang or display your Notan (see our book *An Elfin Book of Spirits* for some spirits you can summon.)

"Spirit come and bless us all
And bless this home from wall to wall
And bless our realm and all within
As we united Elfin win."

(Arvyndase)
"Tari koso nar elsor eli wyl
Nar elsor wyr elum an burk va burk
Nar elsor eli'na êld nar wyl enåver
Tat eli atåraïn Êldat bem."

(Pronunciation)
Tay - rye co - so nair eel - soar e - lie will
Nair eel - soar were e - loom ane bew-k vah bew-k
Nair eel - soar e - lie'nah eald nair will e - nah - veer
Tate e - lie a - tah - ray - in L - date beam.

**VORTEX SPELL:** (for increasing harmony, cooperation and success in your vortex, elven coven)
"As we unite and create this spell
Greater harmony comes as well."

(Arvyndase)
"Tat eli atårey nar talys wyr moja
Raltfa belo kosolu tat darl."

(Pronunciation)
Tate e - lie a - tah - ray nair tay - liss were moe - jah
Rail-t - fah be - low co - so - lou tate dare-l.

**ATMOSPHERE SPELL:** (for affecting the ambience and feeling of a particular place)
"Creativity (or harmony, peace, prosperity or whatever you wish to evoke) will now increase
Continue on and never cease."

(Arvyndase)
"Talyskotu yon mat memarn
Lortyn ton nar konzar orz."

(Pronunciation)
Tay - liss - co - two yone mate me - mare-n
Lore - tin tone nair cone - zair oar-z.

**ABUNDANCE SPELL:**
**"More and ever better still**
**Success doth come just as we will."**

(Arvyndase)
**"Gilf nar vari rilfa vila**
**Reda båver koso oda tat eli yon."**

(Pronunciation)
Gile-f nair vay - rye rile - fah vie - lah
Re - dah bah - veer co - so oh - dah tate e - lie yone.

**ENERGIZING SPELL:** (Use to create greater energy in your eald and make everyone who comes there feel more positively energized.)
**"Electric is the feeling clear**
**Renewing all who do come here."**

(Arvyndase)
**"Jarlor da tae selfdas vyrn**
**Lofadas wyl jae ba koso jän."**

(Pronunciation)
Jayr - lore dah tay seal-f - dace vern
Low - fae - dace will jay bah co - so jan.

**HEIGHTENING SPELL:** (Use for increasing the feeling of Elfin and the sense of magic and excitement in a place and in the individuals there.)
**"Excitement builds ever stronger**
**And it grows as we're here longer."**

(Arvyndase)
**"Aronddir ladlu vari mylthfa**
**Nar ter lythlu tat eli'da jän tisofa."**

(Pronunciation)
A - row-nd - dire laid - lou vay - rye mill-th - fah
Nair tier lith - lou tate e - lie'dah jan tie - so — fah.

**HEALING SPELL:**
**"Healing within, healing without**
**Healing here and all about."**

(Arvyndase)
**"Hyrndas enåver, hyrndas enåkon**
**Hyrndas jän nar wyl basar."**

(Pronunciation)
Herne - dace e - nah - veer, herne - dace e -nah - cone
Herne - dace jan nair will bay – sair.

## Birthing Elfland

Now for larger group art participation, you might wish to play Birthing Elfland or Birthing a New World. We have enjoyed facilitating this art experience with a number of groups in classes we were teaching and, of course, we have also enjoyed this process in our eald with our own elven circle of sisters and brothers. Children enjoy this process as well and add to the magic in playing it with any group.

**The Magical Image:** *The Magic is drawn by the tribe and Elfland is manifested.*

### Materials Needed:

- A large piece of white paper that is 10 feet by 3 feet rectangle. Cut this large piece into odd shapes — 10 to 25 pieces depending on the size of the group, so that each person will have one. This is often called Butcher's paper and can be found in large rolls at Costco and other stores that supply restaurants. Be sure that each piece is numbered consecutively on the back (very important!).
- A large amount of art supplies for drawing and painting, including: paints, colored pens, crapas, paste, colored construction paper, glitter, scissors,

### Directions:

Ask each person to take a few minutes to examine their own personal myth, their awareness of their magical self and find something that they feel is important to bring forth into a world that they might birth together as a group, to manifest Elfland.

Give each person one of the oddly shaped pieces of paper cut from the rectangle. We suggest that you do not gesso the pieces of paper or they will be too heavy and curl (see the next page for photo example). Now with an array of materials in an open studio approach, ask the individuals to use their paper to make an image to bring into the new world, one of a power, an ally, an element, an attribute of their otherkin type, an archetypal energy, a magical being, a totem animal, a natural or technical object, a scene or an abstract drawing, painting, or collage piece.

After the art is completed individually, have everyone come together in a circle and each person then comes to the center, one by one beginning with who ever has the piece with the number 1 on the back, and lays their piece down explaining what they are bringing into the world we are giving birth to. After each person has had their turn to place their piece in order of their number on the back of their piece, everyone stands around the collective map of our new world and circles it (you can have them recite one of the spells at the end of this section as you do so). If you have more than 12 people, you will need to ask them to do the circling in two separate groups, so everyone has a chance to really see the entire creation. After the group members circle their creation and gaze upon the new world, Elfin, Faerie or Elfland or some realm or eald thereof, ask everyone if there is anything that is missing and needs to be spoken into being. Finally, it is important to bless the new world into existence in the lives of all those who participated, as well as in the cosmos. This is an especially powerful group art project for a close group of people who may be coming to the end of their time together and need some closure and a farewell experience together. Of course, it can also be used as an introductory experience to a full moon magic circle.

This Birthing of Elfland project was done with paper that was too thick because we put gesso on each piece, so each curled up and did not have the effect of lying together as one sheet. Still it was beautifully magical!

This second Birthing of Elfland project worked as a whole much better, artistically speaking, because we did not gesso the pieces and they fit together as one sheet, a magical new world manifested.

## Elven Spell Casting

**FAERIE SPELL:** (Use for creating and increasing your ability to have Faerie and its magic and powers all about you and swirling through your life.)
**"Faerie born wherever I look**
**Arising like magic from out of a book."**

(Arvyndase)
**"Farri daend ernvari El shi**
**Valufodas sylar êldon an zes u na lyr."**

(Pronunciation)
Fair - rye day - eend ear-n - vay - rye Eel shy
Vay - lou - foe - dace sill - lair l - doan ane zees you nah ler.

**ELFIN SPELL:** (Use for manifesting the spirit of Elfin in your world and in your life and the lives of your kindred.)
**"Elfin rising in our hearts**
**New world wakens, now it starts."**

(Arvyndase)
**"Êldat luftdas ver eli'na bomli**
**Fae telth siltålu, mat ter altulu."**

(Pronunciation)
L - date lou-ft - dace veer e - lie'nah bow-m - lie
Fay teal-th sile - tah - lou, mate tier ale - two – lou.

**ELFLAND SPELL:** (for blessing or creating a specific place as elven land or as an elfin abode)
**"This place we charge is elven land**
**Where shall abide our elfin band."**

(Arvyndase)
**"Wyr al eli fylre da êldata taru**
**Ern van ruden eli'na êldat darn."**

(Pronunciation)
Were ale e - lie fill - re dah l - day - tah tay - rue
Ear-n vane rue - dean e - lie'nah l - date darn.

**EALD SPELL:** (for your home or eald, your sacred, magical elven space)
**"Energized and filled with love**
**Blessed by the Shining Ones above."**

(Arvyndase)
**"Didaronåïn nar ulåïn ena kyêla**
**Elsorïn la tae Nesedas Atåli usel."**

(Pronunciation)
Dye - dare - row - nah - in nair you - lah - in e - nah kye - l - lah
Eel - soar - in lah tay Knee - see - dace A - tah - lie you — seal.

**VORTEX SPELL:** (Use particularly for blessing and energizing the group its'elf and not just the place that you inhabit together.)
**"Together as one Elfin emerges**
**Our powers increased, our magic it surges."**

(Arvyndase)
**"Eldan tat ata Êldat amlu**
**Eli'na eldroli memarnïn, eli'na êldon ter poshlu."**

(Pronunciation)
"Eel - dane tate a - tah L - date aim - lou
E - lie'nah eel - drow - lie me - mare-n - in, e - lie'nah l - doan tier poe-sh — lou."

## Elven Chess

We have written quite a bit about this elven game in our book *Eldafaryn*, which we think you would love reading if you are interested in our art, games, and elven life style. We have been playing Elven Chess since it was first introduced to us in the 80s by our fae sisters Anodea Judith and Eldri Little Wolf. We admit that we changed the rules a bit to fit our own Elven philosophy and to make the game move along more quickly, making it easy to play with elfae of all ages.

Elven Chess is ultimately a method of making a piece of group art together that reflects some of the magic of the participants. It is an ancient elfin game and unlike traditional chess, this is not a game of competition but rather of cooperation and style. It is essentially creative in nature and it is somewhat like the psychological process called Sand Tray, but rather than silent participation, it involves story telling on the part of the participants. It is designed to teach young elves to cooperate toward a goal with aesthetic values as the guiding principle. The object of Elven Chess is to construct together a beautiful diorama using the playing pieces collected to do so, while letting them express their story and inner truth while doing so.

**The Magical Image:** *Each elf in turn builds a magical land where everyone wins.*

## Materials Needed:

We suggest that you first find a sturdy medium to small size box to keep your treasures in that will be used to play this game. We have been collecting and revising our elven chess pieces for decades and continue to do so to make the game new and interesting each time we play it. In this way, our art is ever evolving with the new elements we add. Each Elven Chess set is unique and we actually have two sets now. Be sure the pieces that you collect are not too large, as they should be easily picked up and placed on a board or on a cloth upon which you are playing the game. You will need to have a variety of playing pieces and at least 30 to 40 to start (50 to 60 is an optimal number, although there really is no limit save your capacity to store the set between uses).

Some examples of pieces are: figurines (fairies, gnomes, elves, etc.), action figures, rocks, stones, crystals, bones, moss, lichen, sticks, plastic trees from play sets or train sets, and any magical items you select. It is left to the elves doing the collecting to include what they feel would work and add magic and beauty to the diorama to be created. We have a small hobbit house, a plaster skull, and a raised metal cobra in one of our sets, so let your imagination be your guide as to the variety of pieces.

You will also need a board or cloth (we always use a cloth but also find that a board under the cloth makes it helpful to move the entire finished game later to a safe place to display it) about three feet by three feet. You will place this in the middle of the table or floor where you are playing and it will be used to set the pieces on as you play the game.

## Directions:

There needs to be at least 2 players, but we have enjoyed playing with many more. Four or five players are ideal. Each elf takes a turn in succession as the game is played in rounds. On their turn they may do one of three things: 1). They may place a new piece on the board or cloth, 2). They may move a piece already on the board, or 3). They may remove a piece from the board. As they do so they tell a story: What, or who, is the piece, and what is it doing, or what is its magical power or purpose. After

having made their move, the game rotates to the next player. When all the pieces are used in the scene, the game is over. We like to leave the art we have all made together out for a few days, and enjoy looking at it, musing over it and even doing oracles about it (particularly the I Ching) as to its magical and more esoteric meaning to our elven group. Above is the an example of a game being played in our eald or elven home, we call Eldafarn, so far only 10 pieces have been played and there is quite a dynamics going on in this magical land!

While doing our practicum hours in a graduate Art Therapy Program, we also had the opportunity to play Elven Chess with many people, and many were not Elfae or at least not Awakened Elfae. We found that everyone loved playing it, even if it was a little difficult for them to say much about their piece each turn. If this occurs, it may help for the person to try to express from their feelings just one word that relates to the piece they have selected. And if you can ask the people playing to add a couple of pieces to the elven chess set before you begin the game, this helps to ease them and motivate them. We have found that children are excellent at collecting pieces for the game. In time, this game can greatly improve ones imagination and ability to verbalize a narrative.

Also, through the process of playing with a number of different groups, we found that it was best if each person had one piece that they picked out from the beginning that only they were allowed to put upon the board, move or remove it. This was especially important for young teenagers, but for some older elfae as well. It gave them a sense of security, which some people need, in an otherwise fluid game flow.


## Elven Spell Casting

**GATHERING SPELL**: (You may use this as you seek and gather your pieces together. Chant this spell and let your elven chess pieces come to you.)
**"Each piece doth have meaning and comes to me now
Speaking the truth of when, why and how."**

(Arvyndase)
**"Cha per båver tir vondådas nar kosolu va el mat
Nordas tae lodver u nas, vas nar po."**

(Pronunciation)
Chah peer bah - veer tire vone - dah - dace nair co - so - lou vah eel mate
Nor - dace tay load - veer you nace, vayce nair poe.

**BLESSING SPELL**: (for charging your elven chess set with magic so that those who play it together gain a blessing by doing so)
**"Each move evokes a magic spell
And blessings rise and around us swell."**

(Arvyndase)
**"Cha ral caltomlu na êldon moja
Nar elsordasli luft nar anabo eli zurd."**

(Pronunciation)
Chah rail cal - tome - lou nah l - doan moe - jah
Nair eel - soar - dace - lie lou-ft nair a - nay - bow e - lie zoo-rd.

**CREATION SPELL**: (for letting the chess game serve as a symbolic movement for truly manifesting Elfin)
**"Elfin bright we now create
For its birth we can hardly wait."**

(Arvyndase)
**"Êldat ilu eli mat talys
Fro ter'na daen eli vek maqi her."**

(Pronunciation)
L - date eye - lou e - lie mate tay - liss
Fro tier'nah day - een e - lie veek may - qwi hear.

**COOPERATION SPELL**: (for creating harmony and arousing group effort toward the common goal of creating Elfin)
**"You move, I move, together we succeed**
**Bringing us all we wish and all that we do need."**

(Arvyndase)
**"Le ral, El ral, eldan eli redae**
**Curådas eli wyl eli felj nar wyl dij eli ba golt."**

(Pronunciation)
Lee rail, Eel rail, eel - dane e - lie re - day
Cur - rah - dace e - lie will e - lie feel-j nair will dye-j e - lie bah goal-t.

## Elven Home or Eald Creation

This is a process we have done with numerous individuals, especially those kindred who have come a long distance to visit us and sometimes stay with us for a few days. Back in 1999, Syleniel and Ashram, some of the first elves to identify thems'elves as being Elenari, came from Texas, where they were living at the time, to visit us and we played this Elven Game with them. It was such a magical manifestation of our elven community! We have also played it with other elven visitors and with members of our 'cohort' in the Depth Psychology Master's Program at Sonoma State University. It is a fun thing to do together, a great icebreaker and sometimes quite revelatory concerning the individuals playing it together.

This process involves creating or designing an Eald or elven home together. When Zardoa had first graduated from Military School (which he likes to call the Linton Hall Academy of Magic) when he was young, he missed his close friends that he had lived with at that boarding school for eight months out of the year for six years. So, he began creating small drawings of the mansion he imagined he would one day own and putting in all the rooms in it where he and his friends would live together. It was, in its way, like a simple architectural design of the interior of a house. And that is essentially what this is, only an elven home.

**The Magical Image:** *The Elves work together to design an elven home to live in.*

## Materials Needed:

- You need a large piece of cardboard, white is ideal. It can also be a large piece of paper, although cardboard lays down better. Still, you use what you can find. For our part, we happened to come upon a dozen or so two foot by three foot white cardboard pieces that one might find in an art store or even in the art section of a large grocery store. We got ours for free; however, we don't even remember whether someone gave them to us or we found them left on a table at the swap meet at the end of the day or what, but we put them to use creating the design for elven homes and using that process to connect with our kindred.
- And, of course, you need pens (colored jellie pens are fun for this project) or markers.

## Directions:

This is easy: Lay down the cardboard or paper on a hard surface, usually on the floor or table, between the people playing. If the floor is carpeted you may wish to find a large size board to put beneath it. Draw a large square, rectangle or whatever, on the paper to indicate the outer walls of your elven home. Draw openings for the outer doors. We usually do at least one on each wall. Add a porch if you want one. And then, one participating elf at a time begins drawing in rooms in the house, usually about three by four inches in size, saying what the room is, such as: "this is my bedroom," or "this is a tarot reading room," or whatever, and describing it and all its beauty, magic and wonder. If you are creating a large room, like a ballroom that will take more than one turn, simply tell the people you are playing with what you are doing and ask that they leave room as you extend the ballroom. Or draw it completely and have it account for two or three (depending on the size) or more of your turns.

Often, those who are new to the game ask us what our budget is in imagining this home we are building together. Our answer always is: unlimited! Let your imagination free and create whatever you will. You will surely wish to do some magic with your final drawing and you may use some of the spells below to manifest its magic.

## Elven Spell Casting

ELVEN HOME SPELL: (Use to create magic through the Elven Home process to manifest a real home like the one you are designing.)
**"We create our elven home
Our base from which to safely roam."**

(Arvyndase)
**"Eli talys eli'na êldata elum
Eli'na fard an tild va della dune."**

(Pronunciation)

E - lie tay - liss e - lie'nah l - day - tah e - loom

E - lie'nah fared (or fair-d) ane tile-d vah deal - lah due – knee.

**BLESSING SPELL:** (to bring blessings upon the individuals who are designing an elven home together)

**"This home a spell by which we're blest**
**With luck and magic, elf friends the best."**

(Arvyndase)

**"Wyr elum na moja la tild eli'da elsorïn**
**Ena niv nar êldon, êlda edarli tae rildor."**

(Pronunciation)

Were e - loom nah moe - jah lah tile-d e lie'dah eel - soar - in

E - nah knive nair l - doan, l - dah e - dare - lie tay rile – door.

**MAGIC ENHANCING SPELL:** (to enhance the power of your magic within your own manifest eald as it exists already)

**"Greater do our powers grow**
**Greater wisdom we do know."**

(Arvyndase)

**"Raltfa ba eli'na eldroli lyth**
**Raltfa zardpos eli ba ken."**

(Pronunciation)

Rail-t - fah bah e - lie'nah eel - drow - lie lith

Rail-t - fah zair-d - posce e - lie bah keen.

**TOGETHERNESS SPELL:** (Use to unite the individuals who are working on the elven home process together and draw them closer together.)

**"Closer you are bound to me**
**Now we go from I to We."**

(Arvyndase)

**"Veskfa le da cyrnïn va el**
**Mat eli tas an El va Eli."**

(Pronunciation)

Vees-k - fah lee dah cern - in vah eel

Mate e - lie tace ane Eel vah Eli.

# Chapter 13 . . . . The Magic Circle
## (Cloth or Drawing on Floor)

One of our favorite ways to perform our magic with a tribe of our elven brothers and sisters is to first spend the time preparing a beautiful Magic Circle, with all the symbols that we wish to use in our magic painted or sewn onto the cloth. The preparation period before a magic circle ritual is perhaps the most important time spent to set the intention of the magic and assure success of your will. We do commit some time to cleaning our eald and the ritual space we plan to use for the magic circle (the purification), but much more of our time is spent on making our art for the magic. (Yes, we elves much prefer creating to cleaning!) This includes making our costumes, our magical instruments, cooking and preparing offerings of food and drink, and also sewing or drawing the magic circle itself, with accompanying symbols and spells written out to be used in the magic.

**The Magical Image:** *The Elven tribe sits on the floor around a magic circle filled with symbols of ancient wisdom.*

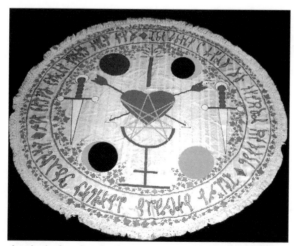

Our magic circle for rituals that we created by painting a tablecloth,
using our magic symbols including the elven star in the middle
and elven script on the outer circle.

## Materials Needed:

- Circular cloth or cloth you cut into a circle.
- Paints and pens, crayons, or other marking tools.
- Embroidery threads and needles if you decide to embroider yours.
- Stencils for ivy or leaves, etc.
- Various rulers and circular objects (such as pans) for drawing the symbols.

## Directions:

For making the magic circle featured on the previous page, we used a circular table cloth that we came upon one time for about twenty-five to fifty cents at a Good Will 'As Is' sale. You can cut an old sheet in a circle or find some other cloth to use. This one has fringe around its edge that we thought was a particularly nice touch.

How you decorate it is up to you. You could embroidery your circle, but in this case we just used acrylic paints that we happened to have around. We will caution you that if you use paints, you will probably wish to put plastic sheeting under it otherwise you will most likely wind up painting the floor as well, like we did.

You will probably wish to draw your symbols on first with soft pencil, chalk, or even crayon.

You may also have noticed the ivy painted around the inner circle. We happened to have some stencils of ivy around, left over from when our daughter was a teenager and wanted us to paint her room with black walls, red trim and blue vines going around it. Which we did. Since the landlord was intending to (and did) tear the house down later anyway, he said we could paint it any color we wished.

## Elven Spell Casting

INVOCATION SPELL: (Use for charging your magic circle with energy and power.)
**"This magic circle does now fill
Enchantment great enacts our will."**

(Arvyndase)
**"Wyr êldon dalso bålu mat ula
Syrandir ralt tadinlu eli'na yon."**

(Pronunciation)
Were l - doan dale - so bah - lou mate you - lah
Sir - rain - dire rail-t tay - dine - lou e - lie'nah yone.

**EVOCATION SPELL:** (to draw particular spirits or energies to your circle)
**"We call, you come most rapidly**
**Our greatest wishes come to be."**

(Arvyndase)
**"Eli koar, le koso erst vapåla**
**Eli'na raltdor feljli koso va te."**

(Pronunciation)
E - lie co - air, lee co - so ear-st vay - pah - lah
E - lie'nah rail-t - door feel-j - lie co - so vah tea.

**BLESSING SPELL:** (Use for putting a blessing upon the magic circle so all who enter it are blest thereby.)
**"Step into the circle bright**
**And all that's wrong will be set right."**

(Arvyndase)
**"Cid verva tae dalso ilu**
**Nar wyl dij'da nårk yon te pånd mard."**

(Pronunciation)
Sid veer - vah tay dale - so eye - lou
Nair will dye-j'dah nark yone tea pond mare-d.

**MAGIC MANIFESTING SPELL:** (Use to increase the power of your circle so using it makes your own powers ever greater and more adept.)
**"Strong now, more powerful, my power will become**
**As I within this circle step and feel its magic hum."**

(Arvyndase)
**"Mylth mat, gilf eldrofel, el'na eldro yon casae**
**Tat El enåver wyr dalso cid nar self ter'na êldon zerm."**

(Pronunciation)
Mill - th mate, gile-f eel - drow - feel, eel'nah eel - drow yone cah - say
Tate Eel e - nah - veer were dale - so sid nair seal-f tier'nah l - doan zeer-m.

**REALM/EALD BLESSING SPELL:** (Your magic circle is the center of your personal Universe and from it you can make all things better and more successful.)
**"From this center outward flows**
**Success, and love as our magic glows."**

(Arvyndase)
**"An wyr concyr zesari shurlu**
**Reda, nar kyêla tat eli'na êldon lums."**

(Pronunciation)
Ane were con - sir zees - air - rye sure - lou
Re - dah, key - l - lah tate e - lie'nah l - doan looms.

**IDENTITY SPELL:** (The magic circle is also your escutcheon, your banner, your flag, the symbol of the sovereignty of your band, tribe, vortex, your people.)
**"We are the fair folk who shine in the night**
**We are the elf (or faerie or other) folk who bring on the light**
**We are the <u>Silver Elves</u> ( or give the name of your group or tribe), the weavers of love**
**Who braid all the threads from the starlight above**
**Who craft in the moonlight and lift those below**
**The way to the future to all we do show."**

(Arvyndase)
**"Eli da tae faer ehar jae glis ver tae sol**
**Eli da tae êlda ehar jae cura ton tae lun**
**Eli da tae Arvyn Êldåli, tae tolsfa u kyêla**
**Jae plyt wyl tae nesli an tae mêllun usel**
**Jae korfar ver tae tarsålun nar ralf dijli yana**
**Tae yer va tae lasel va wyl eli ba teke."**

(Pronunciation)
E - lie dah tay fay - ear e - hair jay glice veer tay soul
E - lie dah tay l - dah e - hair jay cur - rah tone tay loon
E - lie dah tay Air - vin L - dah - lie, tay toal-s - fah you key - l - lah
Jae plit will tay neice - lie ane tay mell - loon you - seal
Jay core - fair veer tay tayr - sah - loon nair rail-f dye-j - lie yeah - nah
Tay year vah tae lay - seal vah will e - lie bah tea – key.

**"If music be your magic**
**And magic be your song,**
**We'll dance the circle round again**
**'Til Elfin bright doth dawn."**

# Chapter 14 . . . . Magic Clothes Closet

Many elven homes have what we call a "Magic Clothes Closet." If you ask the elven spirits, they will help you collect all that you need for just such a closet. And before you know it, no matter how much you seem to take out of a magic clothes closet, it always grows and changes and is full of delightful costume pieces that come to it. Ours is always abundantly full of scarves, satins, lace and frills, gloves, velvets and shimmering clothing of all sorts (anything that glitters) and cloaks, capes, hats, belts, beads, lots of jewelry, and any other beautiful pieces of clothing we might like to add. We use our Magic Clothes Closet for all who would like to dress up for our magic circles and we also let people take some clothes, wear them at our parties, add and exchange.

**The Magical Image:** *The elves and faeries dance around as they select shimmering clothes to wear from a huge Magic Clothes Closet!*

## Materials Needed:

- Clothes of all sorts particularly made of beautiful material like velvets, lace or silks, scarves, belts and belt bags, hats, long satin gloves, capes, boots, sashes, sequined or other fancy shoes. Amulets, pins, talismans and every decorative thing that would make an elven costume. Faerie wings for faeries, elf ears, jewelry, or whatever.
- Oh, and you may need some hangers or shelves or dresser drawers or clothes hanging hooks of all sorts.
- And a place to store them all in which it is easy to get to them, thus a closet, a bunch of boxes, a chest or best of all a room or even your entire house.

## Directions:

Gathering clothes and accessories for a Magical Clothes Closet is easy once you put your magic to work (see our summoning spells at the end of this chapter to use for this purpose), but it goes on forever. Just ask the Shining Ones to help you. Far more than you need will come to you and fill your closet in a very short time, so also be generous with your abundance.

We used to sell used hippie, gypsy, costume, elf and faerie clothes and costumes (along with crystals, incense, candles and do tarot for a $1 a reading) and we would have lots and lots of clothes left over after we had made a good profit on the group we had purchased them with. We had an enclosed porch where we hung these clothes and every so often we'd have a magical elf party, invite all our friends and at the end of the party, we'd give them each a large garbage bag or two and let them fill them with as many costume pieces as they desired to take home.

Even then, we never quite had enough closet space and now that we currently live in a small apartment in Waikiki, our closet is even smaller. However, it is still filled to the brim with costumes, hats, capes, belts and other things and as we have always done we also have belts, sashes, wands, swords, wizard staffs, enchanters' canes, elven stars and other jewelry hanging on our walls, positioned in the corners of our rooms and accessible when we need them. See the following page for an example of some of our scarves hanging on the wall in a large woven bag and a special scarf hook (hooks are as important as shelves in an elven home!). Our apartment is a huge closet in a sense and our costumes are everywhere. We are not sure if that constitutes commitment or insanity but we are sure some folks would think we need to be committed, but we love it. We are nearly always ready to put on our elf ears and to costume up.

So collect everything you can that looks like it may be part of a costume and remember, things that are slightly damaged but still look cool can often to altered to be part of a hat, vest, or some other bit of elf raiment.

And remember, being elven hedgewitches, much of what we get comes freely or very cheaply to us. So, don't forget to give sometimes, too, of things you aren't using that others might like. Spread the magic and attract luck that way.

**"The Elves Say: Some people accuse the elves of being clothes horses, we say we are clothes thoroughbreds."**

## Elven Spell Casting

**SUMMONING CLOTHES SPELL:** (Use to draw good costume pieces to you that you can wear or alter into elven raiment.)
**"Magic threads woven fine**
**Come to me and now be mine."**

(Arvyndase)
**"Êldon nesli tolsta sisan**
**Koso va el nar mat te el'na."**

(Pronunciation)
L - doan niece - lie toal-s - tah sigh - sane
Co - so vah eel nair mate tea eel'nah.

**DRAWING ACCESSORIES SPELL:** (for attracting scarves, swords, belts, pouches or other accessories for your costumes)
**"Belts and hats and sashes, too**
**Everything we need**
**To show our elven flair about**
**The world to magic seed."**

(Arvyndase)
Cyrhelli nar tulili nar vortynli, bil
**"Lotymjart eli golt**
**Va teke eli'na êldata êlm basar**
**Tae telth vah êldon dern."**

(Pronunciation)
Sir - heal - lie nair two - lie - lie nair vour - tin - lie, bile
Low - tim - jayr-t e - lie goal-t
Vah tea - key e - lie'nah l - day - tah elm bay - sayr
Tay teal-th vah l - doan deer-n.

**BECKONING SWORDS, WANDS AND OTHER PARAPHERNALIA SPELL:**
**"Complete my style with stunning grace**
**Awestruck the looks on every face."**

(Arvyndase)
**"Adonyr el'na fås ena juddas darsh
Zelkalkïn tae shili ton lotym fyli."**

(Pronunciation)
A - doan - ner eel'nah fah-ss e - nah jude - dace dare-sh
Zeal - kale-k - in tay shy - lie tone low - tim fill – lie.

**INSPIRATION SPELL:** (to inspire you in creating and putting together a costume or elven outfit)
**"A vision it does come, I see
My elven flair is now set free."**

(Arvyndase)
**"Na jilo ter ba koso, El ten
El'na êldata êlm da mat pånd alo."**

(Pronunciation)
Nah jie - low tier bah co - so, Eel teen
Eel'nah l - day - tah elm dah mate pond a – low.

"Modern elves put on pointed ears and faeries don wings in the same way some folks wear flag pins or team shirts or hats, we are declaring our love and allegiance."

"The Elves say: The true panacea for all ills is Elfin. It heals us, it loves us, it makes us anew, filled with the spirit of all magic true."

"The world is illusion so the elf sages say, make it the most wondrous illusion you may."

"Those who seek to rule by fear and force are ever bewildered and frightened by the elves who seek to guide and inspire using wonder."

> **"If it sings to your soul
> And your spirit alights,
> In the midst of the dark
> It will grant you elf sight."**

# Chapter 15 . . . . Magic Travel Rocks and Magical Elven Runes Stones

Painting rocks and stones has always been a delightful pastime of these elves. We spent some years living near the Russian River in Northern California and during the winter months when there was little rain, we enjoyed walking the dry creek bed behind our house in search of smooth flat rocks. The rocks we treasured looked much like a good throwing rock for playing 'Ducks and Drakes,' which is the official name for skimming stones across water. We used the smaller ones we would find for making our elven rune sets, and the ones a little larger for painting into what we called our Magic Travel Rocks, although we first started this practice of making elven magic rocks and hiding them in our work and other places about in Carbondale, Illinois, when we had the Elves of the Southern Woodlands vortex of the Elf Queen's Daughters. (And, by the way, we —Zardoa and Silver Flame—first met at one of these work places, so the magic rock Zardoa placed there helped bring us together! So be sure and use your magic to meet other elves.) Both sides of the rock need to be flat because we often paint a sigil on one side and elven words on the other side. And, because we take them with us when we go traveling to distant lands, we prefer rocks that are pocket size for our Magic Travel Rocks.

## Magic Travel Rocks

We find that carrying rocks painted with elven symbols and sayings, is perfect for our magic when traveling to distant lands. Besides being easy to transport, carrying them in our suitcase and then in our pockets as we explore a particular area, it is easy to find places to leave them in woodlands and really any hidden place near where we wish to leave magical blessings will do nicely.

**The Magical Image:** *A vortex of traveling elves lay their magic rocks around the four corners of the ancient forest and say their elven blessings for Gaia.*

## Materials Needed:

- Rocks or stones, or tiles.
- Paint and brushes or paint pens and Sealant.

- And, of course, the sigils you create or find to put on the rocks (see our books *The Book of Elven Runes* and *An Elfin Book of Spirits*).

## Directions

After collecting flat smooth rocks, we place them on our magic tables, sometimes for years before we paint them. This way they live with us for a long time and collect our elven blessings. As you can see in the photos below, we paint symbols (sigils, elven spirits, and elven runes) on one side and our magical blessing words on the other side. At the very end of the art process, after painting the rocks on both sides, we seal them with Ceramcoat All-Purpose Sealer that is sold at many art supply stores. This sealer, which unlike other sealants we have tried, does not come off in water, and stays rain or shine, on the rock permanently and does not give off a strong odor when drying.

**Left: Draw out the symbol on paper and paint on rocks**
**Right: Seal painted rocks with Ceramcoat All-Purpose Sealer**

Once the rocks are complete, we place them on one of our magic tables and there they further collect the magic, again, sometimes for years before we take the rocks with us to be placed as elven blessings here and there throughout the world. We have gifted rocks to the spirits of New Zealand (Hobbiton), Australia (south and north), Italy, Japan, Thailand, Belgium, Denmark, Germany, Estonia, Russia, Finland and Sweden, and of course throughout the USA and the Hawaiian Islands, to name just some of their locations.

**Magic Travel Rocks placed on one of our magic tables**
**with the Orb of Healing.**

**Three Magic Travel Rocks that we took with us to New Zealand and Australia:**
**Left: Symbol side, Right: Elfin blessings**

## Magical Elven Rune Stones

We Silver Elves have created our own original set of rune stones (see *The Book of Elven Runes)*. We don't generally use our Elven Runes in the same way we use other oracles like the Tarot or the I Ching, inquiring about day-to-day questions, or inquiries concerning stressful situations, although we sometimes do use them along with these other oracles as an additional point of view. But instead we mostly use the Elven Runes in coordination with some magic we are doing, drawing them on some seal we may be creating, making them a part of an elven magical circle, or using them for some elven artwork we are creating to both decorate and magically magnetize our home. We also love to engrave our original elven runes on magic wands, staffs, and canes that we have created, which makes them beautiful and enhances their magic. Throughout this book, you will find that we have used our elven runes on many art projects (for examples see chapters 23 and 24 on making canes and wands and on making witches' spoons).

**The Magical Image:** *Two wee elven children walk through the woods and find the best smooth stones for making their Elven Rune Stones.*

## Materials Needed:

- Rocks or stones, or tiles
- Paint and brushes or paint pens
- Sealant
- And, of course, runes you create or find to put on the rocks (see our book *The Book of Elven Runes*).

## Directions:

We give complete instructions on how to make your own set of elven runes in our book *The Book of Elven Runes*, so we need not repeat it here. But it is important to say that the first step is to collect the stones that you plan to use to make your rune set and you may wish to begin that process as soon as possible. In the photo on the previous page, you will see that we have used small tiles and you may surely do so yourself. These are identical in form and thus don't have a tendency to favor one over another regularly when throwing the runes. But our original sets are made using smooth creek rocks from our own creek bed that we found with our two children when they were young. However, there is a caution here. While we liked the idea of finding creek rocks, unfortunately creek rocks often have moisture trapped in them and sometimes will break when they are tossed together. So if you use this method you may need some replacement stones. These rocks need to be half the size of the smooth rocks you use for making the magic travel rocks.

While living in Northern California on the side of a creek connected to the Russian River, we would walk the creek bed together each year when the rains were gone and the water was very low and find rocks that had been smoothed by the rushing waters. Just be sure that your rocks are somewhat flat and uniform in size as much as possible. You will need 40 rocks to complete your set and, as we say, at least a few more as spares. You best be getting started on the searching process, which is great fun, we must add.

Of course, you may also wish to make up your own symbols and unique rune set and in that case, be mindful of your dreams because magical symbols often come to us in dreams.

## Elven Spell Casting

SPIRIT SPELL: (Use for instilling a particular spirit within a magic travel rock.)
**"Mighty spirit ( or name the spirit) now appear**
**And make this magic strong and clear."**

(Arvyndase)
**"Jolvath tari mat forno
Nar kord wyr êldon mylth nar vyrn."**

(Pronunciation)
Joal - vayth tay - rye mate for - no
Nair cord were l - doan mill-th nair vern.

**PURPOSE SPELL**: (for creating a rock for a particular magical purpose)
**"Within this stone great power lives
Abundance (healing, magic, or whatever) it now ever gives."**

(Arvyndase)
**"Enåver wyr koln ralt eldro elsarlu
Konåkora ter mat vari luthlu."**

(Pronunciation)
E - nah - veer were coal-n rail-t eel - drow eel - sayr - lou
Co - nah - core - rah tier mate vay - rye lou-th – lou.

**INSTILLING SPELL**: (for instilling magic into your rune set so they will tell you the truth clearly and accurately)
**"The power of the runes awakes
To guide us true for all our sakes."**

(Arvyndase)
**"Tae eldro u tae majili vasålu
Va foren eli lod fro wyl eli'na naruli."**

(Pronunciation)
Tay eel - drow you tay may - jie - lie vay - sah - lou
Vah for - reen e - lie load fro will e - lie'nah nay - rue – lie.

**"The Elven Druids say: Nature creates its own runes. Reading them takes a bit of magic."**
**—Old Elven Saying**

# Chapter 16 . . . . Mojo Bags

Also known as medicine bags, gris-gris bags, juju bags and mojo hand (thus in a sense a hand bag), conjure hand, lucky hand, conjure bag, trick bag, root bag, spirit bag, toby, jomo, charm bag, spell bag and various other names. You place items that you wish to invoke (draw into yours'elf) and evoke (summon to you) that have to do with your personal magic and powers, both actualized and potential, which is to say developing. A mojo bag is like an amplifier of your personal magic power and helps guide the powers you

wish to you. It helps if you carry it around with you regularly, although you could also keep it upon your magic table (what most people call altars) or back and forth — on your magic table to charge it and around with you to dispense its magic as you go about your life. You can carry it in a pocket, or wear it on a belt or around your neck, depending on how it is constructed. Here to the right is a photo of Zardoa's small round mojo bag that he has been carrying for some years.

**The Magical Image:** *The elven shaman wears a mojo bag filled with runes drawn at the full moon gathering and spreads hir magic through the shire.*

## Materials to Collect:
1. A drawstring bag or cloth or leather for making your own bag.
2. Marker for inscribing spells within your bag.
3. String and cord. Needle and thread. Possibly buttons.
4. Optional: Sage, tobacco or other burnable herb for purifying and instilling magic in your bag.

## Directions:
Small drawstring bags are relatively easy to find. We have several in a storage shelf area where we keep most of our tarot decks and books related to oracles. But if you are going to make your own, you just need to have a bit of cloth and fold in along the seams and

sew it together. Then fold at the top so you create another seam, in which you can weave a string, cord or piece of leather through. Then fold the entire back at the center and sew it up along the sides.

You might alternately create a flap that goes over the top and ties or buttons to close the bag.

You can sew on a cord along the sides so it hangs around your neck or two cords so it can tie and hang from your belt.

As it happened, our first mojo or elven spell bag was given to us by our daughter, who had originally, in her Goth period, made it for hers'elf. It was a round leather piece with holes spaced around the outer edge that a leather string had been woven through so it could be drawn together and the contents contained. On the inside of the bag in a spiral going from the outside to the center, she had inscribed a spell in Norse Runes, which due to hir Goth disposition at the time had a bit of a melancholy aspect to it. However, we found that with the alteration of a couple of the rune letters the spell was easily transformed into one evoking prosperity and light.

Alas, after several years of carrying this bag about, it got accidentally left in a pocket of a pair of pants and was washed, making it shrink. However, the contents were still fine and were transferred to a small string bag (also round) that we already had and that Zardoa has carried ever since. In the gentle-time, the previous bag became the hat for Feather, a faun statue that is one of our larger teraphim among the 500 or so in our elven home (see photo to the right of Feather in his mojo bag hat with peacock feather on top).

## Elven Spell Casting

**PURIFICATION SPELL:** (for purifying the bag to receive the magic)
**"This bag is cleansed and open so**
**The magic I charge will in it flow."**

(Arvyndase)
**"Wyr baz da sonlurïn nar caro re**
**Tae êldon El fylre yon ver ter shur."**

(Pronunciation)
Were bay-z dah sewn - lure - in nair car - row ree
Tay l - doan Eel fill - re yone veer tier sure.

**CHARGING SPELL:** (for charging the contents of the bag)
**"Energized and full of power**
**From it our magic spells will shower."**

(Arvyndase)
**"Didaronåïn nar fel u eldro**
**An ter eli'na êldon mojåli yon vere."**

(Pronunciation)
Dye - dare - roan - nah - in nair feel you eel - drow
Ane tier e - lie'nah l - doan moe - jah - lie yone vee – ree.

**DEDICATION SPELL:** (If you are dedicating the bag or its contents to a particular purpose.
You can utilize this spell a number of times to cover various purposes.)
**"Abundance (or healing or enchantment, prosperity or whatever you desire) does this**
**bag now fill**
**And ever after will now spill."**

(Arvyndase)
**"Konåkora bålu wyr baz mat ula**
**Nar vari låka yon mat jurn."**

(Pronunciation)
Co - nah - co - rah bah - lou were bay-z mate you - lah
Nair vay - rye lah - kay yone mate jour-n.

**"The Waters of Elfin flow from its heart into the souls of the Elven."**
**—Ancient Elven Knowledge**

# Chapter 17 . . . . Mythic Cards, Tarot Cards, and Magic Character Cards

We Silver Elves are the first to admit that we do not always make our own cards, and at one point in time, before we made the journey to live in Hawaii, we owned over 50 tarot decks that we had bought new at magic stores and also second hand at swap meets and a number of which had been given to us by our daughter. And while it is surely wondrous to collect all the beautiful cards that you can find and afford, there is something truly magical about making your own mythic, tarot, or magic character cards by using your own images of life and inspired by your own inspirations and illuminated by your personal insights that deeply touches the elven soul.

## Mythic Cards

Mythic cards are very much like collaged soul cards and one may enjoy making them using a variety of images and symbols that are torn out or cut out of magazines. You may also use a graphics program to make your cards. The idea is to create a deck or series of cards that expresses the different elements of your soul, your spirit, your personality and the various aspects or 'faces' of your being. You may think of these as archetypal cards. The idea is to symbolically represent all the elements of yours'elf and your world, your eald and the world around it, especially as you experience it as a magical and mythic realm. In other words, allow your imagination to roam free. Consider the world as it is and as it can be. Create cards to symbolize you, your allies, your otherkin type, the spirits, the Shining Ones, your magical realm, the challenges you face, your powers, and all that lives within it and is linked or associated to it. If you have been wishing to do some art and magic around your past life memories, this is a perfect project for expressing your past life awareness. It may also be used to spontaneously see what comes up in the art around your past lives to help you further develop continuity of consciousness.

**The Magical Image:** *The Hedgewitch expresses the essence of hir soul in a card.*

## Materials to Collect:

- If you are going to draw the cards yours'elf, you'll need colored pens to do so. But we know that many people don't really feel adequate in their drawing skills. However, this isn't about being good at drawing. This is about expressing your inner world, your imaginal world into cards. Even if you can only draw stick figures, you can still do this. Don't judge your art, your drawings, just express yours'elf.

- On the other hand, you may prefer to cut items out of a magazine or collect images you have downloaded from the web and create a collage. You could also use photographs.

- Glue, paste.

- Or you may wish to use a graphics program such as Photoshop and/or Illustrator to put all your selected digital graphic symbols and images together in and make your mythic card on your computer (see the photo below for an example).

- Card stock to print or paste on. And if you are making your mythic card in a graphics program, then you will still need card stock to paste your finished graphic card upon.

**Above is a soul card that Silver Flame made in Illustrator (glued to card stock) around the archetype of the Wounded Healer, which relates to her personal myth. She also found that as she worked on this card, some symbols she felt also related to new awareness of some past lives emerged as images.**

## Directions:

The directions don't really have much to do with cutting, pasting or using a graphics program on your computer. That you already know how to do. The real directions are about looking within yours'elf and seeing what your potential is, who you are destined to be and what your world will look like as you further develop. What is the environment of your inner world and how do you express it into a series of cards so that it is a complete view of your world and covers every part of your magical being and that world that is to be? Do a bit of soul-searching, not morality judgment but a real look at who you are and the direction you are heading toward. Do this soul reflection periodically as you make the cards. In a way, our art is the stage upon which our inner world may delight in expressing itself. These magical soul cards are for you; they do not necessarily need to be shared unless you feel so inclined.

## Elven Spell Casting

INNER SEARCHING SPELL: (Use for looking into your soul in order to understand your inner spirit, nature and powers.)
**"The Truth within my soul revealed
And thus my destined future sealed."**

(Arvyndase)
**"Tae Lodver enåver el'na der sotosïn
Nar hern el'na lawaïn lasel dabåïn."**

(Pronunciation)
Tay Load - veer e - nah - veer eel'nah deer so - toe-ss - in
Nair hear-n eel'nah lay - way - in lay - seal dah - bah – in.

OUTER SEARCHING SPELL: (for seeing and understanding the world around you)
**"The world around is now shown
And every detail will be known."**

(Arvyndase)
**"Tae telth anabo da mat tekeïn
Nar lotym jugyrm yon te kenïn."**

(Pronunciation)
Tay teal-th a - nay - bow dah mate tea - key - in
Nair low - tim jew - grim yone tea keen – in.

ENERGIZING SPELL: (to change and empower your cards)
**"Swirling about and filled with soul
Every part creates the whole."**

(Arvyndase)
**"Mushdas basar nar ulåïn ena der**
**Lotym sun talyslu tae loj."**

(Pronunciation)
Mew-sh - dace bay - sayr nair you - lah - in e - nah deer
Low - tim soon tay - liss - lou tay low-j.

**ENVISIONING SPELL:** (to make your cards an effective tool for divination)
**"Clear my vision, pure my sight**
**Thus I find the path that's right."**

(Arvyndase)
**"Vyrn el'na jilo, nord el'na terad**
**Hern El låc tae tål dij'da mard."**

(Pronunciation)
Vern eel'nah jie - low, nord eel'nah tea - raid
Hear-n Eel lock tay tahl dye-j'dah mare-d.

**MAGIC EMPOWERMENT SPELL:** (so your cards can be used in conjunction with your magic to draw things or people to you or to create or influence certain situations)
**"Each card does great power wield**
**So to my will the world does yield."**

(Arvyndase)
**"Cha maka bålu ralt eldro yot**
**Re va el'na yon tae telth bålu ped."**

(Pronunciation)
Chah may - kay bah - lou rail-t eel - drow yote
Re vah eel'nah yone tay teal-th bah - lou peed.

## Tarot Cards

Of course, you may paint your own original deck of tarot cards, but we have generally used graphic arts for our card images. Silver Flame got a blank tarot deck (available from U.S. Games) and converted it using the ideas that go along with her specific somatic mind-body reflection process on gut feelings. She found that as she interpreted cards in her readings for people that she could more easily flow from her intuition if she could use the language she had developed to describe life experience from a deep gut feeling level. For the images, she used our graphic arts banners (see photo below).

**Five of the Major Arcana Cards of Silver Flame's deck: Top Left: Understanding is Coming Out of Confusion (The Moon); Top Right: You are Shining (The Star); Bottom Left: You Are Being Yours'elve the Elf (The Sun); Bottom Middle: Is There a Knot in Your Gut? (Death); And Bottom Right: They Judged You on What They Saw of You, Not What You Felt (Devil).**

Here is our point however, in creating a tarot deck, especially an elven or faerie tarot deck, it is not a matter so much of making different pictures as a direct substitution for the Waite-Rider deck or the Crowley deck, etc. but of understanding the cards from your own life view and philosophy and expressing that understanding on the various cards. This will help your readings greatly. You won't have to be looking up what the cards mean, if you are just learning, if it is expressing your own philosophy and understanding of life. And remember that a tarot deck can be made using any theme that interests you (see our book: *The Voice of Faerie: Making Any Tarot Deck Into an Elven Oracle*).

**The Magical Image:** *The Elven Diviner shuffles hir cards and lets them spring from the deck.*

## Materials to Collect:

Like the soul cards, you may wish to draw the images yours'elf or collect images to collage or gather images you can put together in a graphics program.

You will need card stock of some sort. You can buy blank tarot cards from U.S. Games or some other company, or you can get blank 3' by 5' filing cards, or you can get card stock and print on it.

## Directions:

The directions are the same as the soul cards, but there are a few things to consider.

First, if you get blank tarot cards from U.S. Games or wherever or you use 3' by 5' index cards, you will probably be gluing the images on (if you don't draw them directly on the cards yours'elf) and this can make the cards bulky.

We had a faerie friend who made her own tarot deck and sent us a copy and the sealant she used would stick some of the cards together at times and that can be a problem. However, we know from having done over 75,000 readings that even professionally made tarot deck will get thicker with use. The plastic like film will gradually peal off, and the cards will expand and wear out in time anyway. When we were doing readings professionally, we bought a new deck every couple of years.

Zardoa made his own deck using photographs sealed onto card stock (see photo below) but it has that same bulkiness. We encountered a man who owned a metaphysical shop in Hawaii the first time we went to visit there, before we relocated to Hawaii, who wanted to show us the deck he made and it had the same problem. So if you are using a sealant on them, make sure it is one that won't become sticky with moisture from the atmosphere. Still, if you are gluing the images on, it is still likely to be bulky.

Zardoa's Deck: Are you already wondering about the holes in the top left of each card? Those are there because Zardoa used this deck at times at an outside swap meet to give readings and he pinned them to a board as he read so the wind would not blow them away. Thus our "Holy Cards!" Left Card: Camouflage, Blending With Our Surroundings, Ace of Success (Discs); Top Middle: There are No Doors In Faerie, Enter (The Last Judgment); Bottom Middle, Once Upon A Time, Remember (The Hanged Man); and Top Right: Suspense, Waiting For a Sign, 7 of Ideas (Swords).

Instead of using sealant, you may also have your cards laminated at the print shop or check into buying your own laminator, which is something we have done recently and find it very cost effective, as well as convenient.

If you don't get cards that are already cut and are the same size, which is to say if you use a graphics program and print the cards on card stock several to a page, it is nearly impossible to get them cut to the same exact size, even if you take them to a print shop to have them cut. Small print shop cutters press the cards together and wind up cutting at a slight angle. This is just to say that if you make your own cards, they may not be perfect, but even professionally done cards wear out in time anyway. Still, having your own deck that expresses your personal philosophy can be wonderful in so many ways.

And, of course, there are also several 'Make Your Own Personalized Tarot Deck' websites (print for a fee) that our elfae kindred have used for printing (see: https://www.makeplayingcards.com), which you may wish to try.


## Elven Spell Casting

**EMPOWERING SPELL:** (to charge and vitalize the cards)
**"Alive and filled with energy**
**Potent you shall always be."**

(Arvyndase)
**"Alsaru nar ulåïn ena didaro**
**Mamer le van verat te."**

(Pronunciation)
Ale - sayr - rue nair you - lah - in e - nah dye - dare - row
May - mere lee vane veer - rate tea.

**SEEING SPELL:** (for its divinatory uses)
**"I know and in the knowing say**
**The truth declared and the way."**

(Arvyndase)
**"El ken nar ver tae kendas des**
**Tae lodver serytïn nar tae yer."**

(Pronunciation)
Eel keen nair veer tay keen - dace dee-ss
Tay load - veer sear - rit - in nair tay year.

MAGIC MANIFESTING SPELL: (for using the tarot cards for magic)
**"Power in these cards awakes
Transforms the world for all our sakes."**

(Arvyndase)
**Eldro ver wyrli makali vasålu
Jorqumlu tae telth fro wyl eli'na naruli."**

(Pronunciation)
Eel - drow veer were - lie may - kay - lie vay - sah - lou
Jour - que-m - lou tay teal-th fro will e - lie'nah nay - rue – lie.

## Magic Character Cards

We created a set of cards that were similar to *Magic The Gathering* Cards. In fact, at the time we did this, we didn't have any graphics programs in which to do them as a complete whole, so we took photos of our friends and cut them out and glued them on to *Magic The Gathering* Cards, and made up little things about the individual, such as Elven Ranger, etc. and typed it up and pasted it over the card.

**A Magic Character Card we made of our selves, Zardoa and Silver Flame,
and call it "Weldlinque: Summon Elves"**

Now, you might think that we just wanted some of our own cards and ideas to play with when playing *Magic The Gathering*, but that was not the case. Rather, this was an exercise designed to help awaken Elf Sight and our elfin intuition. All of Faerie exists in disguise so to speak all around us all the time. But we usually view the world in the enculturated fashion and from the preconceived notions that have been inculcated into us from when we were little children and slowly told that our magical view of the world was wrong. Doing these cards is meant to help reawaken that magical point of view and to increase our ability to see the world in all its elfin glory.

We started with various elf friends and acquaintances that we had at the time, took their photos and began making the cards. We always asked the person what their kin type was, which is to say we inquired if they were an elf, faerie, gnome or whatever. We did this by saying to them, if you could be anything, be any type of person in a Fairy Tale, or one of Tolkien's books, or some other fantasy tale, what would you be? The answer quite often turned out to be rather surprising. We asked this question of a lovely young woman we knew that we thought might be an elf, but she turned out to be most emphatically a dwarf. An incredible graphic artist of our acquaintance told us he was a troll, a gentle troll, however, not one of those unkindly folks often encountered on the Internet "trolling."

We always accept what the person tells us as being sacrosanct. We don't second-guess them. What they say about their inner imaginal and spiritual s'elves and natures is what goes. The fact that they may not have achieved this as yet in reality is only to say the Path to Elfin goes ever on and we are ever becoming.

However, sometimes we would come across someone who simply had no idea of what they are spiritually speaking and we would give them some choices or possibilities to choose from if this was the case. Or if they were totally stumped, and only then, we might pick something out for them, our best sense of what they are and see how they reacted to it. Their reaction will tell you nearly everything for the truth is concealed in their feelings about thems'elves and if you say that you think they might be an elf and they frown, keep making suggestions until something clicks. You'll at least get in the general area this way and from that you can create your card. Of course, *Magical The Gathering* cards aren't just characters, they are also powers, places and other elements and here your intuition is vital to create your own Magical Character Cards. You might ask a place what sort of magic and energy it holds, but it will be responding through your experience of the area and your intuition.

If you create enough of these cards, so that they pretty much cover everyone you know and every significant part of your immediate environment and surrounding area, filtered through the Vision of Elfin, you will also have a rather nice tarot like deck you could use for magic or for divination about your immediate life.

**The Magical Image:** *The Wizard pulls a card from his pouch and magic unfolds from it.*

## Materials to Collect:

You will need photos of your friends (it's great if they are in costumes), acquaintances, and places in your environment, such as your house or apartment or nearby stores and restaurants, etc. See them through the eyes of magic. You can also collect images from the Internet to represent people and places in your life. Think Elfin, think Faerie, imagine your world as it exists within Faerie or Elfin.

## Directions:

A graphics program would surely be the best way to do this, but if you don't have one, cutting and pasting on to *Magic The Gathering* or similar cards or just 3' by 5' index cards will work as well. Create your Faerie or Elfin realm and include all aspects of it, even those things or people that obstruct you or may challenge you. And don't forget yours'elf and your closest ones. Or if you are alone at this time, imagine those who are to come into your life, who you desire to be in your life and create cards for what they will be like as elven or fae or otherkin individuals to draw them to you. What do you imagine they will be like? What sort of elf kin do you need and desire? Or create shadow cards that represent those people or elements that will appear in your life but will prove surprising in some way —people or things that represent the mystery and the unknown. You can create cards for them and fill in their details when they actually arrive.

## Elven Spell Casting

ELF SIGHT SPELL: (Use to increase your Elf Sight and to see Faerie and Elfin as it exists in the world around you.)
**"I see Elfin (or Faerie) all around**
**The truth of magic now is found."**

Arvyndase)
**"El ten Êldat wyl anabo**
**Tae lodver u êldon mat da låcïn."**

(Pronunciation)
Eel teen L - date will a - nay - bow
Tay load - veer you l - doan mate dah lock – in.

MAGICAL EMPOWERMENT SPELL: (to fill the cards you create with magical power)
**"Great the powers you possess**
**Will bring to me the very best."**

(Arvyndase)
**"Ralt tae eldro le horva**
**Yon cura va el tae lefa rildor."**

(Pronunciation)
Rail-t tay eel - drow lee whore - vah
Yone cur - rah vah eel tay lee - fah rile – door.


**DIVINATION SPELL:** (for using the cards to see the past, the present situation and the potential future)
**"Tell me, show me, make it so**
**The cards reveal what I would know."**


(Arvyndase)
**"Fram el, teke el, kord ter re**
**Tae makali sotos wu El yonta ken."**


(Pronunciation)
Frame eel, tea - key eel, cord tier ree
Tay may - kay - lie so - toe-ss woo Eel yone - tah keen.


**UNDERSTANDING SPELL:** (Use for clearly understanding your cards, the people represented by them and the situations that appear.)
**"I see the world and understand**
**With wisdom and a guiding hand."**


(Arvyndase)
**"El ten tae telth nar neha**
**Ena zardpos nar na forendas aro."**


(Pronunciation)
Eel teen tay teal-th nair knee - hah
E - nah zayr-d - pose nair nah for - reen - dace air – row.

**"If the world were a deck of playing cards, elves would be the wild cards."**

**"Elves sometimes refer to morning dew as Earth Rain."**

**"To the Elves, Santa Claus is a great elven lord. How do we know he is an elf? He's surrounded by elves! How do we know he's a great lord? He gives gifts so generously! Who but an elf would be joyously surrounded by elves? And who but a great elven lord would give so much without asking for anything in return? Except perhaps that you re-gift as generously as you got and live in the elven spirit of the holidays." —Old Elven Wisdom**

# Chapter 18 . . . . Painting

Just like writer's block, many elves (and others) are afraid to even begin to paint and do not think of themselves as having any artistic ability, although truly all elfin folk have, at the very least, some latent artistic ability. The truth is too often we just have had very little education and encouragement in art and never have had a chance to develop our talents. If you have had limited past experiences making art and feel nervous and unsure when faced with a blank canvas, remember that this is normal because you are stepping out of your artistic comfort zone.

Fine arts painting is like all creative arts, it just takes a lot of practice to become accomplished at it. But there are a few simple tips that can help you get a good start toward successful painting. So just take a few deep breaths and follow these four tips for beginning painters:

1.) Be sure you have good art materials to work with including a good set of brushes, real canvas, and a good quality of acrylics, watercolors or oil paints. Those cheap poster paints and paper that you may have used as a child in school most likely did not give you a fair chance at painting something you would like and enjoy. We suggest starting with at least student grade acrylics, as they are easier to work with than oils. Watercolors are also fun! Try the watercolor pencils, as they are easy to draw with and use to fill in the color, giving you more sense of control over your painting as a beginner. With watercolor pencils you draw and them wet with a thin brush the lines you have drawn and the color spreads outward.

2.) There are no "mistakes" that cannot be fixed! Once you begin painting with acrylics, just keep adding paint, layer after layer, and if you are not satisfied with how something looks then paint over that part, again and again if necessary. Often times the "mistakes" we paint over lend an added depth of variety to the color background of the finished painting.

3.) Plan to paint many sessions for each painting and take your time! You do not need a lot of time every day, just 20 to 30 minutes. Taking time out of a busy day for small sessions of painting works best if you have your easel and painting set up all the time in a corner somewhere in your house. Then it is there for you to go to for short sessions anytime of the day or night.

4.) Shake out your hands often so not to clinch the brush, which can make a painting look too stiff. Remember to breathe! Enjoy the process!

And, a bonus tip: You may wish to take some art classes at a local college or community college or sometimes through art stores. This may cost you a bit, but the tips you learn can improve your skill immensely.

**The Magical Image:** *The Elfin artist spreads paint on hir canvas with delight.*

## Materials to Collect:

- Canvas board
- Acrylic paints (buy at the least one tube of each of the primary colors, and black and white)
- A number of sizes of good quality brushes
- Large plastic cup for water
- Rags and Drop cloth (we use an old shower curtain)
- Gesso
- A charcoal pencil and water color pencils

## Directions:

Because we had absolutely no fine arts classes to fulfill the prerequisite requirement of the Sonoma State Art Therapy Program that we were both admitted to in 2005, we were required to take a number of classes at the local community college in the studio art department while simultaneously going full-time to graduate school. While it was a lot of work to be in both schools at once and also working at the same time, it actually turned out to be delightful because we truly loved the Santa Rosa Community College classes. The technique for painting from a photo that we will explain and demonstrate (see photo on left) is one we were taught in these studio art classes and it was the single most important technique that we still use today for many of our paintings.

1.) Your first step is to take a clear color photo of something that you desire to paint. You will be attempting to make a painting that is exactly the same as the photo, with of course all the artistic liberties that you wish to make from your own sense of reality and imagination and s'elf expression. These techniques are meant to set you free not limit you.

2.) Once you have the photo that you desire to paint, you will need to scan it and print out the digital copy of the photo on 8 by 11 inch paper. Now using 1-inch squares, make a grid all over the photo (see image on previous page). The purpose of the grid is to help you draw the photo onto your canvas. The grid will be transposed onto the canvas and will give you a guideline to keep your drawing that is underlying your painting to be proportionate.

3.) Now, select your canvas size. We often paint on a 2 feet wide by 3 feet high canvas, because we like big paintings and because it is easy to transpose the grid to the canvas, with a simple ratio of 1 to 3, meaning for each 1 inch square we will pencil in a 3 inch square. Whatever the size of the canvas that you select, you just need to figure out the ratio, that is to say how much to increase each grid square on the canvas so that you have the same number of squares on the canvas as you do on the photo paper.

4.) Now, before you draw the grid on the canvas, we suggest that you Gesso it once or twice, followed by a light wash in some color of your choice. Gesso is a sort of primer for artistic painters. The Gesso will be painted over, but will help assure that all places on the canvas have some color and no stark white is showing. The Gesso will help the canvas so it doesn't soak up so much paint and thus it helps conserve your paint.

5.) After your undercoats are dry, you are ready to draw the grid onto your canvas. Use a light charcoal pencil for the grid.

6.) Once your grid is in place, you are ready to begin drawing what is on the photo onto the canvas (see photo on previous page). You may wish to practice on some drawing paper first. We suggest that you use watercolor pencils for your drawing. Charcoal pencils are also fine to use. Remember that the grid lines will help you draw your sketch proportionately. You can compare just where each item you draw appears on the paper by comparing the grids. In the painting, each square on the canvas is three times larger than each grid square on the photo printed 8" by 11". Using this technique, you will have less trouble getting the figures to look proportionate to reality. Silver Flame used this technique for this painting shown to the right, as a second attempt. She found in her first attempt, without the use of the grid as a guideline, that it was very difficult to draw the peacock body and head in the correct proportions. But with this technique, she was able to draw them out over the grid in her first try. This is a great technique to use if you are a beginner at drawing but would like to do some realistic looking painting despite your lack of drawing skills. On the right is Silver Flame's final painting of the peahens in our back yard.

7.) You are now ready to begin painting. Paint from dark colors to light colors and try to have as much variation of colors and hues as possible. Remember, you will need many coats of paint and can paint over anything that does not suit you.

This is a technique that is useful for both beginning painters and those who are more advanced in skills. Zardoa has used this technique for some complex paintings that he first drew from a photo of a digital collage he made using a number of images he collected. You may have seen some of these paintings as covers on some of our Silver Elves books. Some of our favorites are also hanging on our walls in our eald, including the painting on the left by Zardoa Silverstar for the cover of The Silver Elves' book *Eldafaryn*; subject of painting is the doll by Sharon Aur.

Other paintings that Zardoa created using this same process are on the covers of *Magic Talks* (see photo on the next page), *Sorcerers' Dialogues*, and *Discourses on High Sorcery*.

**Painting by Zardoa for cover of *Magic Talks*.**

## Elven Spell Casting

DRAWING ABILITY SPELL: (to increasing your drawing skills)
**"My skill increasing every day**
**Growing better in every way**
**Every brush stroke confident**
**Creates the image that I meant."**

(Arvyndase)
**"El'na teld memarndas lotym lea**
**Lythdas rilfa ver lotym yer**
**Lotym hoft mynd syndeldir**
**Talyslu tae tolec dij El vondåïn."**

(Pronunciation)
Eel'nah teal-d me - mare-n - dace low - tim lee - ah
Lith - dace rile - fah veer low - tim year
Low - tim hoe-ft mend sin - deal - dire
Tay - liss - lou tay toe - leek dye-j Eel vone - dah – in.

**INSTILLING SPELL:** (Use to instill your painting with magic so those who view it will be enchanted in a particular way.)
**"As you view this painting fair**
**You will be transported there**
**And all the magic I intend**
**Into your life will now descend."**

(Arvyndase)
**"Tat le sant wyr martdas faer**
**Le yon te jorconvïn norn**
**Nar wyl tae êldon El manod**
**Verva le'na ela yon mat gadan."**

(Pronunciation)
Tate lee saint were mare-t - dace fae - ear
Lee yone tea jour - con-v - in norn
Nair will tay l - doan Eel may - node
Veer - vah lee'nah e - lah yone mate gay – dane.

"May star shine light your path even in the midst of day." Olde Elven Saying wishing that one will be guided by the Shining Ones even when one is enmeshed in the hustle and bustle of the world.

"Elves don't do magic to manipulate the world and their environment so much as for the pure joy of enchantment, not that the world doesn't need a nudge in the right direction now and again."

"Elves can be hard to understand but easy to trust, for while their motives often seem mysterious, their friendship is ever steadfast."

"The Elves say: It is never too late to be your true s'elf. In fact, the older you get the more likely you are to give up the pretensions of the world and just be who you have always really been."

# Chapter 19 . . . . Drawing and Painting
## Illuminated Magical Circles

We elves love to draw and paint magical circles, often using florescent glow-in-the-dark paint. We put them up in our bedroom and when the lights are turned out at night, the magic glows lulling us into the enchanted realms of Faerie and Elfin in peaceful slumber.

The image on the right is featured on our Arvyndase book cover. It is also made with florescent illuminating paint and is one of four magic circles that we have created for our longevity and immortality magic. This circle represents the element of fire. We also have one for Earth, Air and Water (each hanging on different walls in our bedroom and thus facing different directions) but they are not painted with illuminating paint. This Fire Longevity Circle has its spells written in Sylvyn Script around the outer circle and in Arvyn (Arvyndase) Script within the elven star. In

between the star points are some of our elven runes (see our book: *The Book of Elven Runes*).

Besides using the dictionary of over 30,000 words in Arvyndase, we have three Arvyndase scripts that may be used with the language as well: Arvyn, Sylvyn and Wizard's Scripts [see our book *Arvyndase (Silverspeech): A Short Course in the Magical Language of the Silver Elves*]. You will find that we use both Arvyndase and the three scripts for most of our art requiring spells.

Another one of our illuminating circles is shown on the following page in the directions section. It is a magic circle bringing elven folk together and we call it 'The Elven Gathering.' The spell is written in Arvyndase.

**The Magical Image:** *The magic glows from the walls in a darkened room.*

## Materials to Collect:

- Coffee or black tea grounds (optional)
- Poster or other paper or canvas.
- Acrylic and florescent paints and brushes

## Directions:

We used brown paper for the circle on the right, 'The Elven Gathering' magic. One of our former housemates left us with dozens of these sheets that are about two feet long and a foot and a half wide and we still have more that we haven't gotten around to using as yet. We like to tear them along the edges for an uneven look as though it was painted on an animal pelt or something. But we have also painted these magic circles on canvas board. We mostly use what is available to us. Again, we are elven hedgewitches. You could also do it on plywood or whatever you may have about or can find cheaply.

But what is nice about the paper sheet is that we took used coffee and black tea grounds (Silver Flame drinks a cup of coffee each morning and Zardoa has Masala black tea, which is black tea with milk and spices), put water in them, boiled them up again and then poured them onto the paper, first using the tea and then the coffee. It gives it a nice stain for a background. Of course, after letting the coffee and tea water set on the paper for a day, we pour off what is left and let the paper dry before painting on it. Also, if some of the coffee or tea grounds fall on the paper just leave it; it makes a bit of a darker stain and that will give it good contrast.

Then, using pots or pans or whatever circular object we had around, we drew the magic circles, used rulers for the lines, and so on and then painted them with acrylic paint and then went over that paint with florescent paint, although the circle shown above, we just used florescent paint. It looks really cool when we turn on the lights at night to go to sleep. You might notice that our images are a bit askew. If absolute symmetry is important to you that you will surely make great effort to get everything exact, but we like it being just a bit off kilter.

We have also used this image shown above for a cover of one of our books, with an addition of using Photoshop filters that made it seem like it was an ancient rock carving (see *Elf Magic Mail, volume 1*). You may have noticed that we turn much of our magical art into book covers.

## Elven Spell Casting

**CHARGING SPELL:** (Use to fill your painting with magic and enchantment.)
**"To its depth this magic goes
And from its core this magic flows."**

(Arvyndase)
**"Va ter'na dorwyn wyr êldon taslu
Nar an ter'na dor wyr êldon shurlu."**

(Pronunciation)
Vah tier'nah door - win were l - doan taslu
Nair ane tier'nah door were l - doan sure – lou.

**ILLUMINATION SPELL:** (for sending out magic as your circle glows)
**"Shining magic bright to be
All are blest whose eyes do see
And when this light is hidden, still
Its magic will fulfill my will."**

(Arvyndase)
**"Glisdas êldon ilu va te
Wyl da elsorïn ja'na arli ba ten
Nar nas wyr lun da rimta, vila
Ter'na êldon yon felu el'na desutra."**

(Pronunciation)
Glice - dace l - doan eye - lou vah tea
Will dah eel - soar - in jay'nah air - lie bah teen
Nair nace were loon dah rhyme - tah, vie - lah
Tier'nah l - doan yone fee - lou eel'nah dee - sue – trah.

**"The Elven Way is simple and true, we do what is best for us and for you."
—Old Elven Saying**

# Chapter 20 . . . . Elven Magic Boxes (Reliquaries)

Reliquaries are containers for the relics of saints. Every sanctified altar in the Catholic faith is said to contain the relic of a saint. Reliquaries, in a sense, are a form of Necromagery, a way of using the sacred magic of the Saints or Shining Ones who have passed on from human form to infuse our own lives with potency.

The word relic, however, has also come to mean things that have been left over from the past, things that are ancient and old. At the same time, when people get the autograph of a famous person or a bit of their clothing, or some other item they owned or were associated with, like their guitar, they are, in a sense, collecting a relic. However, creating reliquaries has become a more psychological art process for putting things, or images of things that are or were important to you, the sacred moments of your life, we might say, into a box that is also a piece of art.

We elves don't have saints, exactly, but we do tend to have Shining Ones and mythic and fictional heroes, such as Tolkien's Galadriel, or Shakespeare's Titania and Oberon and so on and we have aspects of our own past lives as elves and elfae that we cherish and in doing so can create a reliquary of a sort that expresses our love and connection to those beings and things. In a certain way, it serves as a reminder of what is important to us, our values and ideals, our visions and aspirations and our memories of significant magical experiences.

So Reliquary may not be quite a right word for us. Maybe we should call it an Elven Magic Box or a Spirit Vessel or something like that, but the process remains essentially the same. And that is to express what is magical and perhaps sacred in our lives and to let that energy radiate outward spreading the magic wherever the Magic Box display/art may be.

**The Magical Image:** *A Magic Box projects energy from its place on a shelf.*

## Materials to Collect:

- A box, just about any box will do. You can buy blank wooden boxes at art supply stores, but you could also use a cigar box or one of the wonderful decorated wooden boxes from India that some people use to store their tarot cards or their pot stash, or any small cardboard container box will do. They are easy to find and we could go about our apartment right now and probably find at least a half dozen candidates. You may wish to collage, paint or otherwise decorate the interior and exterior of the box before filling it.

- Collect images or small objects that remind you of the major magics and developments in your elfin life and your progress on the path.
- You may need glue or possibly wire to put it all together.
- Paint and brushes, if your Magic Box requires them.

## Directions:

Find an appropriate box and decorate/paint it inside and out if you wish. You may wish to have a specific theme around which you create a scene in the box. For instance, the 'Christ being born manger scene' that is often in front of Christian churches around Christmas is a rather large example of this idea. Of course you may wish to have your theme center around a special magical event or special day in your life, an important vision you have or a numinous dream you had, or anything truly important to you. Or you may wish to simply choose from your feelings with no special theme in mind and place items in your box simply according to what feels right at the moment and calls to you in a magical way. Once you put it all together, be sure to set it up someplace on a wall, or on a shelf or dresser top, magic tabletop or as an art installation.

**Here is a magic box we made like a s'elf portrait. It now sits on a
living room shelf radiating vibrations to guide us on our Elven Way.**

## Elven Spell Casting

**REMINDER SPELL:** (To be used to remember what is really important in your life and your magical and spiritual development and progress.)

**"Every magic moment recalls itself to me**
**And I do now remember my elven history."**

(Arvyndase)
**"Lotym êldon onst lokorlu tereln va el**
**Nar El ba mat narwa el'na êldata talso."**

(Pronunciation)
Low - tim l - doan ohn-st low - core - lou tier - eel-n vah eel
Nair Eel bah mate nair - wah eel'nah l - day - tah tale – so.

**INVOCATION SPELL:** (to inspire you to continue on the path and create even greater events, milestones and memories)
**"The magic I have done grows stronger every day**
**Inspires me to greater acts upon the Elven Way."**

(Arvyndase)
**"Tae êldon El tir båïn lythlu mylthfa lotym lea**
**Felilu el va raltfa dinli repton tae Êldata Yer."**

(Pronunciation)
Tay l - doan Eel tire bah - in lith - lou mill-th - fah low - tim lee - ah
Fee - lie - lou eel vah rail-t - fah dine - lie reap - tone tay L - day - tah Year.

**EVOCATION SPELL:** (Use to evoke inspiration magic into the lives of others who happen to view your artwork.)
**"The magic swirls, becomes greater yet**
**As your eyes upon this set**
**And thus inspired you proceed**
**Your inner s'elf to fully feed."**

(Arvyndase)
**"Tae êldon mushlu, casalu raltfa nov**
**Tat le'na arli repton wyr pånd**
**Nar hern feliïn le murfan**
**Le'na verfa eln va fella gif."**

(Pronunciation)
Tay l - doan mew-sh - lou, cah - say - lou rail-t - fah know-v
Tate lee'nah air - lie reap - tone were pond
Nair hear-n fee - lie - in lee muir - fane
Lee'nah veer - fah eel-n vah feel - lah guy-f.

# Chapter 21 . . . . Elven Fantasy Maps

We just like making fantasy maps sometimes. Decades ago, Zardoa worked in a print shop running printing presses. Among the miscellaneous things one found around the shop was paper that was blue on one side that was used for photocopying architectural drawings. This usually came in long sheets and one day Zardoa found a sheet that some of the chemicals used in the shop had spilt upon and so it had been discarded in the trash. However, when he looked upon it he saw that the chemicals in reacting to the paper had created what looked like three islands with mountains on them surrounded by blue water. He took the paper home, added names for elven villages on it and hung it on our wall for years.

This was not his first love affair with maps, however. When he was very young he loved to read and study history. All sorts of history. At military school, he would even read through the entire history book for his year and then read the next year's text. His favorite historical period, however, was the American Civil War, also known in the South at that time as The War Between the States. He had a huge book about this conflict in which his favorite things were artist's maps showing battlefields and the positions of various troops upon it. He would pour over these for hours. Maps just fascinated him as they do many elves.

You can see this same love in the proliferation of maps of Middle-earth that Tolkien created. Obviously, he was also a map lover. And clearly many other folks, who love Tolkien's works, are so as well. Maps commonly accompany fantasy novels. They help the writer, as well as the reader, understand the region sHe is writing about.

However, instead of planning out our maps, we like to have them created in a somewhat accidental or serendipitous fashion, just like the map Zardoa found at the print shop. And we do this with the same technique we've mentioned previously of collecting our used coffee and tea grounds, re-boiling them and then pouring them onto thick paper and letting it sit for a while and seeing what landmass is created by this process. You may think of other ways to do it, or you might be a planner wishing to map it all out in your head first. Or you may be a writer and just wish to create a map to see the places you've already created in your mind and in your story. But whatever the reason you wish to do this, if you love creating maps of your inner world, we offer you in the direction section of this chapter some simple suggestion for doing so based on what we have done.

Scroll making is similar. You just need to imagine what your scroll is about. The materials are the same, but you may wish to check out a book on calligraphy if you wish to get fancy, or you can always use Tolkien's scripts or our Arvyndase scripts, such as Arvyn, Sylvan and Wizard scripts or use the Arvyndase language itself for writing your scroll (see our books *The Complete Dictionary of Arvyndase* and also *Arvyndase (Silverspeech): A Short Course in the Magical Language of the Silver Elves*) or one of Tolkien's elven languages. Our Elven brother Anadae used to write us letters in English but wrote the English so it resembled the script on the One Ring, which looked really amazing. Just make your scroll look as ancient and wonderful as possible. The hardest part for most people will probably be figuring out what you want it to say.

**The Magical Image:** *The elven wizard studies a map intently.*

## Materials to Collect:

- Paper or some other surface for your map.
- Inks, acrylics or other paints, or coffee and tea grounds or other coloring or dyeing plants and herbs. Possibly sharpies.
- Your imagination.

## Directions:

Of course, you can, as we suggested just pour out the watered coffee and tea grounds or some other coloring agent (for instance you would use watercolors, or acrylic paints that have

been watered down so they are very thin, fluid and like watercolor), and see what comes up, but you can also just draw the outline of the world you have in mind. Many of our maps are very simple imaginary fantasy worlds we paint using the method we just described, see the map of the "Island of Åvåndale" shown in the photo above. And on some occasions, we have painted our maps on a paper that did not turn out to show up well, so we turned it into the background for a symbol painting that we placed over the map (see photo to the left). In that way, the map makes am interesting background and adds a layer of esoteric meaning to the painting. This circle (see previous page) is also one of the four magic circles we painted for our longevity and immortality magic that are hanging on the four walls of our bedroom (see chapter 19). This one represents the element Earth and has a double infinity sign (as a sign of immortality) in the middle that forms a four-leaf clover, so it also is for good luck.

However, consider this idea as well. What if you took an actual map of the area where you live and then created your own map based upon that map, transforming the area into Elfin or Faerie just as you did, in a sense, by creating your own *Magic The Gathering* cards, using as a technique for enhancing your Elf Sight abilities. Small towns sometimes do this creating local maps for tourists with various shops and monuments and so forth being highlighted. Only, in this case, you are viewing your local area from your inner vision and saying to yours'elf, if this is or were Elfin, what would be here and there and so forth. See Elfin or Faerie overlaid on your local town or immediate area.

Now, if you decide to do that, consider scanning a local map and then taking the map and taping it to a window (unless you have a light box) and then taping the paper you are going to make your map upon over it and tracing the essential details. The reason for scanning the map is that most maps are printed on both sides so it is just easier to see what you are tracing if it is only one sided. Now, make you map and transform it.

These are just simple suggestions because, again, we are elven hedgewitches and do things on the fly for the most part. But, there are a lot of good books on making fantasy maps and D&D maps and so on that you can get if you are deeply into map making.

Sometimes we outline the landmass of the map using a brown sharpie pen, which looks pretty cool, although we are not fond of using sharpies, or paints, or even cleaning supplies or any other tool that gives off fumes and a chemical smell. Our glues, sealants and other things we use give off very little chemical order or fumes. However, somebody gave us a whole bag of colored sharpies for free, so occasionally we use them, although we expect we could get the same effect with acrylic paint or a thick tipped calligraphy ink pen. Still, we tend to use what is available around us for the most part.

We actually once knew and spent a good deal of time with a faerie couple who lived in our area whose job at that time was selling maps of various sorts to public schools. Also, the male of the faerie couple would make his own maps with an eye to selling them in the future. He told us that almost every mapmaker creates a fantasy street in his map (or a 'blind') so sHe will know if someone else copies hir map and claims it to be hir own. So, if you have ever driven around some place you are unfamiliar with and found some street on the map that doesn't actually exist in reality, as these elves have, that's the mapmaker's signature, as it were.

## Elven Spell Casting

**REALM SPELL:** (To be used for inspiring your vision and your understanding of the worlds that you are creating.)
**"Show me true with Elven Sight**
**The world that is by Faerie Light."**

(Arvyndase)
**"Teke el lod ena Êldata Terad**
**Tae telth dij da la Farri Lun."**

(Pronunciation)
Tea - key eel load e - nah L - day - tah Tea - raid
Tay teal-th dye-j dah lah Fair - rye Loon.

**RE-ENVISIONING SPELL:** (for seeing the world you live in, in a new elfin light)
**"Reveal to me the truth to see**
**The world that is and will now be."**

(Arvyndase)
**"Sotos va el tae lodver va ten**
**Tae telth dij da nar yon mat te."**

(Pronunciation)
So - toe-ss vah eel tay load - veer vah teen
Tay teal-th dye-j nair yone mate tea.

**FASCINATION SPELL:** (Use for capturing the attention of those who view your map and sparking their imagination.)
**"Seeing this your interest caught**
**Calls to your soul all you have sought."**

(Arvyndase)
**"Tendas wyr le'na cathtyn fyskaïn**
**Koarlu va le'na der wyl le tir hedïn."**

(Pronunciation)
Teen - dace were lee'nah cah-th - tin fiss - kay - in
Co - air - lou vah lee'nah deer will lee tire heed – in.

ॐ

## Chapter 22 . . . . Seaweed Pod Rattles

The thing is, in order to create seaweed pod rattles, you need seaweed pods, which means not only being near an ocean but near an ocean that produces them. We used to live in Northern California not far from the coast and these seaweed pods would wash up on the shore regularly. However, we now live in Hawaii, very near the beach, and we've never seen one in the decade+ that we've lived here. But, there is an alternative, which we will get to in a bit.

We used to have an elf friend named Jay, who was an amazing graphic artist, who could draw wonderfully realistic color drawings of pheasants and other birds, who showed us how to make these pod rattles. So thanks and credit due to you, dear elf brother.

When we were in graduate school in Depth Psychology, we made a bunch of these rattles and put them on the floor of the classroom one day and let the other members of our cohort (as they called our master's program group) pick the rattle that called to them. It was quite a lot of fun to see who picked which one. This could also be interesting to do in a magical circle of elfae kindred.

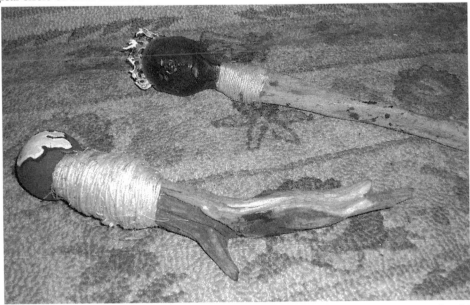

**Shaman rattles we made from seaweed pods. Because they are made form seaweed, which has a high content of salt, these rattles are excellent for protection magic.**

**The Magical Image:** *The elven shaman shakes hir rattle and evokes the spirits.*

## Materials to Collect:

- Seaweed pods, alternately leather, or whatever you happen to think of that will work, like a tennis ball.
- Glue and small balloons
- Sticks, rope, twine or string
- Paint for decorating
- Small stones, gravel or pea beans or garbanzo beans.

## Directions:

If you live near the sea where these seaweed pods wash up on the beach you are in luck. There are seaweed strips like ribbons that come out of the pod on the top, while from the bottom of the pod a long whip like appendage extends. You can often see children along the beach using it as a whip for fun. However, once it dries up it shrinks and is at first slimy and then just a crusty flat string with sand and sea salt on it. The pod itself may or may not collapse. Because of this, we started cutting off the whip part, which we would have to do later anyway, and putting a balloon inside the pod and filling it with just enough air or water to keep it round as it dried. Later, after the pod has dried you will pop the balloon and pull it out. Caution: You don't wish to fill the balloon so much that it splits the pod.

You could make a rattle with leather, as the First Nations peoples did, but for one thing, we're vegetarian and try not to use leather or fur unless it comes to us for free and then we think it is rather disgraceful to the animal that died not to use it. And two, having had access to a lot of seaweed pods, we didn't need to use leather and have never done it this way, but we are certain you could find directions for doing so online, if that is your desire. However, you can also use a tennis ball instead of a pod, even an old one that is slightly broken will probably work if the tear isn't too large.

You will wish to test your chosen handle or stick by inserting it into the pod, just to get the right size stick. So, gather a lot of possibilities of sticks and see which one fits best in the pod but also make sure it fits well and comfortably in your hand. You don't want one that will be irritating if you hold it for a long time.

Once your pod has thoroughly dried and is hard and you have popped and taken out the balloon, you probably want to paint it (or the tennis ball), put sigils or other symbols upon it and then use sealant over that. Use at least three coats of sealant. Let each coat dry between applications. If you want you can save this part to last. If you are using a tennis ball, be sure you use enough paint to cover up its telltale seams. We don't want it looking like a tennis ball. And let's fact it, tennis balls, while easily available, are not as cool as seaweed pods, or puffballs, or some other round ball-like thing you can find in Nature.

You will need to put the gravel or garbanzo beans or whatever into the pod or tennis ball so that when you shake it, the rattle will create a nice rattling sound. You may wish to experiment with different beans or gravel or vary the amount you put in to create different tones. Remember, these elven shaman rattles are essentially maracas and you can get a pair of maracas and paint and adorn them with spirit glyphs, which is an even easier way to go about this, although we like the energy and magic of making our own.

Seaweed pods come with a natural extension, the whip like end that you cut off, so if you leave just a short piece, about an inch or two, this will help secure your pod unto your stick/handle, which you can then wrap with a bit of string or twine around it to further secure the pod to the handle.

If you are using a tennis ball, you need to cut a hole that your stick will fit in easily but not to widely. You want a close fit. And you may wish to poke holes on either side of the opening and insert knotted cord that you then slip through the holes and glue along the sides of the stick for a short distance to help secure the ball to the handle. Either way, glue the pod or tennis ball to the handle and then smear glue down the handle for an inch or so and wrap the twine or cord around the handle and around the glue from the ball or pod downward, but usually not so far that your hand will be in contact with the twine when you hold and shake your rattle. If you haven't already, paint and seal your pod or ball and once everything is done, rattle away and draw the spirit world closer.

## Elven Spell Casting

SUMMONING SPELL: (Use for inspiration as to what symbols, sigils, glyphs you should use.)
**"In my mind the symbols rise
That will this rattle energize."**

(Arvyndase)
**"Ver el'na car tae zyrvåli luft
Dij yon wyr taka didarona."**

(Pronunciation)
Veer eel'nah car tay zer - vah - lie lou-ft
Dye-j yone were tay - kay dye - dare - roan – nah.

CHARGING SPELL: (for charging your rattle for effectively calling the spirits)
**"Spirits upon my vision wake
Empower this rattle that I shake."**

(Arvyndase)
**"Tarili repton el'na jilo sil
Tåeldro wyr taka dij El ronk."**

(Pronunciation)
Tayr - rye - lie reap - tone eel'nah jie - low sile
Tah - eel - dro were tay - kay dye'j Eel row-nk.

# Chapter 23 . . . . Magic Tools:

## Plates and Shields, Chalices, Athames, Wands, Canes and Staffs

lves truly like to make our own magical tools whenever possible. Of course, we are always delighted to accept magical gifts we cannot make so easily ourselves, like knives and other cutlery that we might use in our magic rituals. But we feel that the tools we make with our own hands are the most powerful in our magic. They are certainly filled with our personal energy and enchantments.

In a traditional tarot deck, the plate, pantacle and the shield all represent the energy of the suit of pentacles or coins or earth energy; the wand, cane or staff represent the energy of the suit of wands or fire; the knife or sword represent the energy of the suit of swords or air; and the chalice or cup represent the energy of the suit of cups or water. Note that some systems have the attributions for air/swords and fire/staffs switched, having swords as fire and wands as air. You can decide for yours'elf what works best for you.

## Plates

The magic plate is a small version of your magic circle, which its'elf is a smaller version of your world and your Universe, your magical eald of Elfin, your demesne, your elven home. This is your world in miniature — a symbolic representation of the field and range of your magic and your ability to affect the world. This represents your home, your castle, your magical aura manifest upon the material plane.

Decades ago, Zardoa was teaching a class in the meaning of the tarot at Shaman's Drum in Guerneville, CA., and one class project was to create a magic plate (relating to the disc, pentacle, coins suit). We made one as an example, instilling it with magic (see photo to the right). We cherished that magic plate for years in a house that we had lived in for over a

decade and then one day one of us accidentally dropped something that fell on the plate and shattered it. We knew this was a sign indicating a big transformation in our lives and we suspected that we were going to be asked to move. And in fact, within a few weeks the landlord came and gave us notice due to the fact that he planned to tear down the old house we were living in and build a new, more modern ranch style house for his aging parents to live. We were sorry to see our plate go and to have to move, but we created another magic plate that we have brought with us from place to place as we migrated to better and better living situations.

**The Magical Image:** *At the center of a magic table rests the magical circle inscribed on a plate.*

## Materials to Collect:

- A dinner plate or a platter, depending on what is available and how big you wish this representation of your magic circle/seal to be.
- Paint, we use acrylics but that is up to you. And, of course, brushes.
- Sealant.

## Directions:

The big challenge for most individuals is designing the look of your magic circle that will be represented on your plate/platter. Does it have two circles around it, like a traditional ceremonial magic circle? One on the outer edge probably and one on the inner rim. Perhaps it has Elven or Norse runes between them, or perhaps a spell in Tolkien's elvish or in our elven language Arvyndase.

What is the color of the background? You will be painting that first. Does your circle have a seven-pointed elven star at the center, or an eight pointed Chaos magic star, or perhaps a pentacle or other symbol, maybe a tree or a leaf, or ivy vines, or perhaps a wolf, or dragon or hawk? Does it have swords upon it, or cups, or wands or some other glyphs and symbols?

So, design your magic circle and then paint it on the plate or platter. If you don't feel good about your drawing skills, think simply, think symbolically and download the various elements of the circle from graphics on the internet, arrange them together as you wish on the plate, glue then down, and then use a sealant. We always use sealant on what we paint as well; this helps your art to last much longer.

## Elven Spell Casting

**EMPOWERMENT SPELL:** (for charging and enchanting your magical plate or platter)
**"My realm reflected in this seal**
**Every aspect of my life will heal."**

(Arvyndase)
**"El'na êld musthiïn ver wyr daba**
**Lotym onparo u el'na ela yon hyrn."**

(Pronunciation)
Eel'nah eald mewce - thigh - in veer were day - bah
Low - tim ohn - pay - row u eel'nah e - lah yone herne.

**PROTECTION SPELL:** (for securing and protecting your eald)
**"Ever safe within my eald**
**Potent magic securely held."**

(Arvyndase)
**"Vari del enåver el'na ald**
**Mamer êldon yaderla gospïn."**

(Pronunciation)
Vay - rye deal e - nah - veer eel'nah ale-d
May - mere l - doan yeah - deer - lah go-sp – in.

**PROSPERITY SPELL:** (for increasing financial success and attracting abundance into your life and your world)
**"All I wish does now appear**
**All needs are met, my path is clear."**

(Arvyndase)
**"Wyl El felj bålu mat forno**
**Wyl goltli da cumoïn, el'na tål da vyrn."**

(Pronunciation)
Will Eel feel-j bah - lou mate for - no
Will goal-t - lie dah come - moe - in, eel'nah tahl dah vern.

**HEIGHTENING SPELL:** (for using your eald as an amplifier for your magic)
**"Ever stronger my magic grows**
**Potent magic from here flows."**

(Arvyndase)
**"Vari mylthfa el'na êldon lythlu**
**Mamer êldon an jän shurlu."**

(Pronunciation)
Vay - rye mill-th - fah eel'nah l - doan lith - lou
May - mere l - doan ane jan sure – lou.

## Elven Warriors' Shields

The shield is another magic circle but it is specifically dedicated to protection, shielding, warding and the declaration that you have a right, duty and the willingness and ability to protect yours'elf, your eald and your people. It is your Coat of Arms, your escutcheon. Ancient peoples from all over the world, including First Nations peoples, African tribes and many other peoples, have used such shields. Even modern police still use shields. Here, however, it is not simply a means of protection but a magical symbol of our people, of who you and they are as elves, fae or other and your determination to preserve your/our culture in the present and into the future (see the book *Seven Arrows* by Hyemeyohsts Storm for beautiful inspiration for First Nation's Peoples shield types).

**The Magical Image:** *The Elven Warrior uses his shield to pass through dangers, making time and space interchangeable and achieving unity with his environment.*

## Materials to Collect:

Years ago, like a couple of decades, we came across a shield, a magic shield. It had been left on a table at the swap meet where we set up a weekly shop of our own called the Elven Gypsy Boutique selling hippie, elven, gypsy clothes, incense, crystals and doing tarot readings for $1, quite a deal really, and it brought us a lot of luck over the years. Anyway, someone had somehow stretched canvas, like you use for painting, over a circular dowel rod.

The creator, whom ever it was, had painted it black, put Norse runes in silver upon it and hung Mexican coins from strings with horsehair attached to it. It was pretty cool and we had it on our wall in our eald for years.

But, here's the thing, we have no idea how they got the dowel rod into a near perfect circle. But if you know how, then you can do that and use canvas for your shield. But you can also use the circular cardboard that comes from the back of a large or extra-large pizza. To the right is a shield that we made from a pizza round, decorated with fringe and an elven intuitive sigil.

Or you can use an old plastic or aluminum trashcan lid, which has the addition value of having a handle, like an actual shield, on the back. Naturally, we prefer the aluminum over the plastic but we use what we find. Or you can cut it out of wood, such as plywood sheets.

Or make it any other way, you can figure out how to do it. Although, if you can come across a round metal concave snow sled shaped like a flying saucer, that would be perfect. They often even have handles on the inside like a shield.

You will need paint, also. We use acrylic and bushes, of course. But you could use house paint or anything else you come across or have lying around. You will need sealant. Even if you use acrylics, which are plastic, you may still wish to seal your work over to make it last longer. In the period when the sealant is drying is a good time for some of your spell casting.

And, of course, you will need your own idea of what your shield will be. Take a look at Irish or Scottish family crests. And it doesn't have to be circular, we just happen to like the circular form. Even those tribes that have come to be known as Celtic often had rectangular shields with circles and swirls upon them.

**Two more of our shields made from pizza rounds. Left: A shield with a protection spell written in Arvyndase Script; Right: A shield with a prosperity spell.**

## Directions:

As ever, designing your shield will be the most important part. What does it have on it? An animal totem? A sword? Bow and arrows? Stars? What? And what color is it? Next, find your base shield, trashcan lid, pizza circle, or whatever. What do you have around or can get easily that you can make into a shield? And remember, it doesn't have to be circular unless you really want it to be. Then, make your shield. Add whatever accessories make it aesthetically pleasing and hang it on your wall or wherever.

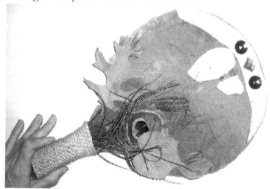

Above is a photo of our shield we made from a paddle. The paddle is excellent as a shield for knocking something forward. Or it may be used magically for knocking negative forces back upon themselves. Our elven sigils are drawn upon it, although we used a light pencil so they are near invisible.

## Elven Spell Casting

**WARDING SPELL**: (To be used to ward off dark magics that are being leveled against you and yours.)
**"No power can our eald invade**
**Our light repels the darkest shade**."

(Arvyndase)
**"Kon eldro vek eli'na ald saron**
**Eli'na lun vosorlu tae dasdor dasa."**

(Pronunciation)
Cone eel - drow veek e - lie'nah ale-d say - roan
E - lie - nah loon voe - soar - lou tay dace - door day – sah.

**POWER SPELL**: (to empower your realm and make it strong)
**"Ever stronger we become**
**As our magic eald does hum**
**United our enchantments weave**
**Greater magics to conceive."**

(Arvyndase)
**"Vari mylthfa eli casae**
**Tat eli'nah êldon ald bålu zerm**
**Atåråïn eli'na syrandirli tols**
**Raltfa êldonli va aronil."**

(Pronunciation)
Vay - rye mill-th - fah e - lie cah - say
Tate e - lie'nah l - doan ale-d bah - lou zeer-m
A - tah - rah - in e - lie'nah sir - rain - dire - lie toals
Rail-t - fah l - doan - lie vah a - roan - nile

**SECURITY SPELL**: (To be used so your people feel safe and secure within the eald.)
**"Feeling safe within this eald**
**Like a baby by its mother held."**

(Arvyndase)

**"Selfdas del enåver wyr ald
Sylar na nysa la ter'na madon gospïn."**

(Pronunciation)
Seal-f - dace deal e - nah - veer were ale'd
Sill - lair nah niss - sah lah tier'nah may - doan go-sp – in.

# Chalices

Chalices represent relationships, especially our relationship to the Divine Magic, the Spirit World and our loving and harmonious relationships with each other. One drinks the water, or communion liquid, that is in the chalice and thus invokes, takes within the energy and power of the Divine, of the Magic, and in that way draws closer to Elfin and one's kindred.

Chalices are not only the receptacles of the sacred waters of Nature and the spirit world, but they are transformative vehicles for trans-mutating or transubstantiating mundane water into enchanted water. Chalices symbolize our ability to be transformed by and through love and our association with other, particularly more evolved, kindred.

**The Magical Image:** *The elven magician lifts hir chalice toward the sky in honor of the Shining Ones.*

## Materials to Collect:

1. If you are a potter you can make a chalice yours'elf. But even if you don't have experience in pottery you can get self-hardening Sculpey polymer clay and construct your own chalice.
2. Or, you may, like us, find chalices or beautiful wine glasses to use.
3. Paint, brushes or an engraving tool.
4. Possibly sealant, but you have to consider if you make your own Sculpey polymer clay chalice and seal it, will the sealant give off toxic elements once it has dried and you have liquid in your chalice. So choose your sealant carefully if you decide to make your own.
5. Optional: talisman, cabochon crystals or other gems.
6. Glue and glue gun.

## Directions:

Make your own chalice, or take your wineglass and paint your own runes or spirit glyphs and symbols upon it, or engrave them if you have an engraving tool (see our books *Arvyndase (Silverspeech), The Book of Elven Runes* and *An Elfin Book of Spirits*). We have an engraving tool and we find it helps if you put the symbol on first in pencil or sharpie and then engrave over it. And engraving can take a bit of practice. Also, leave the inside of the chalice as is so you can drink from it without dealing with the sealant issue.

You could also glue on a talisman of some sort or some crystal most likely in cabochon form. In the photo to the right, you can see that we glued beautiful cabochon gemstones on a cut crystal-like drinking glass that makes a beautiful chalice. Next we glued on a jewelry piece of a 'winged heart' to complete the love magic of the chalice. Bags of cabochon gemstones and crystals may be bought quite inexpensively on the Internet and it is so simple to glue them on and make an entire set of water goblets or wine glasses into beautiful chalices to use in your next elven starlight magic circle.

Although, you may note that at some parties, where the wine glasses are all similar, little talismans are tied or wired to the stem so one can distinguish one's glass from others. So you could also tie a talisman around the stem for a bit of extra magic. Just a thought.

So, the question is what symbol or glyph or rune or spirit sigil would represent your connection to Elfin and your kindred? What energy do you wish to evoke?

## Elven Spell Casting

**CONNECTION SPELL:** (Use for increasing the connection to your kindred.)
**"Strong the bond that draws us close**
**Our family union is foremost."**

(Arvyndase)
**"Mylth tae ellani dij omhyrlu eli vesk**
**Eli'na elpa atådur da larnerst."**

(Pronunciation)
Mill-th tay eel - lane - nigh dye-j ohm - her - lou e - lie vee-sk
E - lie'nah eel - pah a - tah - dure dah lair-n - ear-st.

**COMMUNION SPELL:** (To be used for increasing your link to the spirit world or Nature or the Divine Magic overall.)

**"The lights of Elfin within me shine
My soulful spirit to refine."**

(Arvyndase)
**"Tae lunli u Êldat enåver el glis
El'na derfel tari va losis."**

(Pronunciation)
Tay loon - lie you L - date e - nah - veer eel glice
Eel'nah deer - feel tari vah low – sighs.

## Athame or Dagger

There are few of us who are able to forge our own swords, daggers or athames (ritual knife). However, it is easy enough to find an old or extra kitchen knife around and adapt it to our needs in various ways.

While we will be giving you some other ideas as well on how to decorate your dagger, below is a photo of an example of an elven ranger dagger that our elven kin made from a kitchen knife and leather. There is a piece of leather over the handle with fringe coming out and hanging from the back of the blade. While he surely made this adapted blade for a frontiersman look or a First Nations appearance, it also is very much in keeping with the sort of Wild Elves, called Squirrels, that one finds described in the Witcher series of books and the video game.

**The Magical Image:** *The Elven witch raises hir athame toward the air evoking the elementals.*

## Materials to Collect:

- A knife
- Paints and brushes or an engraving tool or both.
- Sealant.
- Leather or faux leather.
- Leather cord or other heavy cord for wrapping the handle
- Possibly some cabochons or other small talismans.

## Directions:

You may first wish to decide if you are going to wrap the handle and, if so, do that first. Wrapping the handle with cord will make it easier to grip if it is anything but a wooden handle, but be sure and do not wrap it too thick. And if it is a wooden handle, wrapping is not necessary unless you like the aesthetics of the cord.

Now that your handle is wrapped (or not), you can paint runes or spirits sigils or other magical symbols on the blade or handle of the knife. If you paint them on, you may also wish to use sealant. This should help preserve the runes and symbols and yet will still let you sharpen the knife-edge if you wish to do so since the runes are going to be on the wide sides of the knife.

Alternately, you can engrave runes and sigils on the blade (or unwrapped handle) if you have an engraving tool. And, if you don't, you can try using a nail or some other hard, pointy metal object and scratch them in anyway. Be sure to put your sigils on in sharpie, soft graphite pencil or some other form first so you know approximately what it will look like before you start scratching. This may not be fancy or refined, but it is still magic.

Remember, there is a line in the Wilhelm Baynes translation of the *I Ching* that states that as religious (and thus magical observances) progress they tend to become more and more fancy and elaborate; but that the Spirits, thus the Divine Magic and the Shining Ones, look to and care about the sincerity of the offering rather than how fancy it is. Make your magic real and sincere and your athame, and other tools of magic, will be filled with power, no matter how primitive artistically they may appear to be to you or outsiders.

You could also put a cabochon or some crystal or mineral over the little metal piece that often connects the handle to the blade. Frequently, there are three such metal pieces, on each side. However, keep in mind that it may be uncomfortable if you put them where your hand will grip the knife, so secure them behind or in front of your grip, or possibly on the end as a pommel. We prefer knives with wooden handles rather than plastic, but that is up to you and what is available.

## Elven Spell Casting

AIR SPELL: (for instilling the element of air in your athame)

**"The power of the air infused
In the blade that I will use."**

(Arvyndase)
**"Tae eldro u tae eron zorvåïn**
**Ver tae cryste dij El yon nos."**

(Pronunciation)
Tay eel - drow you tay e - roan zoar - vah - in
Veer tay criss - tea dye-j Eel yone knowce.

**POWER SPELL:** (for empowering your athame with the ability to protect you and your circle)
**"By this blade I will secure**
**My eald so it will long endure."**

(Arvyndase)
**"La wyr cryste El yon yader**
**El'na ald re ter yon tiso talos."**

(Pronunciation)
Lah were criss - tea Eel yone yeah - deer
Eel'nah ale-d re tier yone tie - so tay – lowce.

**DISCRIMINATION SPELL:** (for using your athame as a power to discriminate between what is true or false)
**"Keen and sharp as is this blade**
**The working of my mind is made."**

(Arvyndase)
**"Reb nar narl tat da wyr cryste**
**Tae norfdas u el'na car da kordïn."**

(Pronunciation)
Reeb nair nair-l tate dah were criss - tea
Tay nor-f - dace you eel'nah car dah cord – in.

## Magicians' Wands, Enchantresses' Canes, and Wizards' Staffs

We Silver Elven folk love to make wands, canes and staffs. In fact we love it so much that we have been making them for decades. In fact, we love wand, cane and staff making so much that when we have parties or magical gatherings for our elven sisters and brothers, we like to have an entire room set aside where willing participants can go and make a wand, cane, or staff at any time. It helps to have in your wand/staff/cane making room a large selection of sticks, sitting room and floor space, and ample materials for making the wand (see section on materials to collect on the following page).

**Art Room set up for magical wand and staff-making during an elven party.**

The key to success in any group art process — and certainly in wand making — is to have so much assorted available materials that elves can pick from in making their wands that it feels like Christmas! Having the feeling of awe at the sheer amount of glittery and beautiful trinkets and materials available to freely use will offer possibilities that intrigue the imagination, and it is the first step in the creative process.

The generous abundance of having so many beautiful materials to choose from, offers one a sort of awesome feeling of open possibilities that briefly overwhelms one's logic and thus our "functional fixedness" (as psychologist have called it) that keeps us looking at things in the same comfortable ways. And displaying these available materials in a sorted (using boxes, baskets, and other containers) but somewhat random fashion allows people to pick through and enjoy the treasure hunt to find their chosen art materials.

In this way, abundance and surprise and a bit of chaos is the first step (or what Dr. Daniel Goldman, known for his theories on emotional and creative intelligence, coined "The Preparation Stage") that generates fresh ideas in life and, in this case, is the beginning of the creative process that sponsors the creating of magical wishing wands. Also, the suspension of disbelief that is required in making a "Wishing Wand" or "Intention Wand" will bring even the unawakened elfae closer to their true inner nature.

## Materials to Collect:

- A variety of sizes of sturdy sticks, some short enough for wands (from 1 foot to 18 inches long), some three to four feet in height for canes, and others tall enough for staffs (5 to 6 feet). We prefer redwood, willow, holly, ash, all types of driftwood, but any sturdy stick (dead wood not green) that you find on the ground will work. Our Devil's Claw wand (featured in the photo on the right) was made using a piece of driftwood, which often works nicely because driftwood has so many interesting holes to stick gems and other magical items in, as we did with the devil's claw seedpod at the top of this wand. Just after a windstorm, and particularly early during the growing season, is a great time to collect your sticks. For the elves, there is no best time in the moon cycle to collect the sticks for magic wands except for the time that you actually find one, which is to say when we feel the time is right we  go out and look, but we also pick them up if we just happen to come across one or more that look like likely candidates. So we always keep an eye out, no matter where we are for sticks for our future projects. Remember that a curve at one end of the stick can be both very useful and beautiful for a cane or staff. You may choose to scrape the bark off or leave some on for a more natural look. If you plan to carve a rune or spirit name into the stick, you will need to scrape off the bark, so have carving knives handy with other materials.

- Yarn of different colors, lace, string, rope, and most importantly a lot and possibly variety of cords!

- Thin copper or silver wire and wire cutters

- Leather pieces, scraps

- Regular fabric glue like Tacky Glue and glue gun and glue sticks

- Scissors

- Fur scraps (faux or real fur found discarded) and velvet strips

- Stick on jewels, sequins, and some glitter

- Bells

- Crystals and stones of all sizes and types
- Small pouches
- Feathers and shells and silk flowers
- Acrylic paints and brushes
- Carving knives (use for carving on runes and sigils)
- Charms and odd jewelry pieces and shiny things

## Directions:

We elves do not have strict rules on art making in general and certainly not on making wands, canes and staffs. Pick the time in the month, the moon phase, to make your wand, cane or staff that you feel has the greatest creative impact on you personally. For many elves this is near or on the full moon or right before the new moon. But your inner feelings will guide you. There are no should or should not's when it comes to what can be put on your wand or staff. Sometimes, elves select not to put anything on the stick at all and just keep a wand in its most natural form. Ultimately, your wand or staff is a conductor of your magic and so one needs to create them from within your own heart and soul. We simply put forth the materials and space to do the art and let the individuals' instincts guide them.

We only say, "Make it beautiful in your own eyes so that it becomes a part of your inner magic."

The photo to the right is over 40 years ago (yes, we have been making wands, canes and staffs a long time!) and here we have a staff that we made using as a top ornament a piece of wood we found in the forest near our eald. The wood piece looked much like an animal skull and we used our staff in our elven Earth magic for healing and regenerating the forests.

**Magical Image of the Wand**: *The magicianist waves hir wand through the mists and the veil is lifted that divides the inner and outer realms.*

Some of our favorite wands are these elaborate Faerie wands that we made with beautiful flowing ribbons and yarn and silk flowers and leaves. (Left) Fairy sister Michiko with her Butterfly Wand (Right) Zardoa with his wand to open the Elven Realms.

We have our wands all over our elven eald, hanging on the walls, on magic tables, on top of shelves in holders we have made as in the Devils' Claw Wand pictured on page 184, and some in holders on our desks. The wand in the photo below is one that we created using a quartz crystal wrapped with wire at the pointer end. The handle on the other end is wrapped with embroidery thread and we also used the embroidery thread to have tassels to hang from it. There is an enchanted spell painted in silver and outlined in red in Arvyndase Script along the shaft of the wand. This wand is one that we hang on our bedroom wall with our longevity magic.

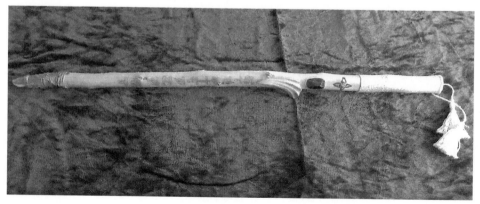

Left: An assortment of wands we have made that sit in a holder on top of Zardoa's writing desk; Right: A wand made by an elven queen attending one of our parties.

We make wands out of anything that looks like it will work. One of our favorite elven magic wands is pictured above and made from a found object. We found a wooden chair that broke and had a beautiful spoke from the back that we could turn into a wand. When something breaks, we see it as a chance for the object to evolve its energy further and also it is often an opportunity for us to harvest materials for making magical tools! It was broken in such a way that the wider end where the handle would be was broken at a 45 degree angle that came to a point. So we sawed it off half way down the break and turned the sawed off piece around so that it fit the broken end, and then glued it in place to make a complete piece. This wand has a moonstone on the handle end and a word of elven magic in

Arvyndase script painted on it, with a seven-pointed star and three crystals in the middle. At the point end of the wand we glued in a beautiful piece of citrine.

**Magical Image of the Cane**: *The elven enchanter uses hir cane to attract a warm glow of light returning to earth.*

**Here Zardoa holds one of our favorite canes made for Lupa, our sister who explores being a wolf therianthrope in her book *Otherkin*. This cane is adorned with a scrap of fur that we had found left in a free box at our community store and had held onto for about seven years awaiting just such a fitting magic.**

We think a word here about the use of fur in our magical items is important. We, like many elves, are against the slaughter of animals for their fur as we are, for the most part, against eating them when it is not necessary to do so. However, we understand that in the past people had to kill animals and wear their fur to survive in harsh weather conditions.

While we don't buy fur to wear or use for our art, we do sometimes wear or use fur for art projects that we have obtained at flea markets and *as is* stores, sometimes thrown away at a swap meet. We feel in a certain sense that it is dishonoring the animal to let their fur be discarded completely and we do find fur beautiful. Often, we just hold onto the fur for years until we can incorporate it into some elfin costume or magical art that we are making, like the cane for Lupa on the previous page.

**Magical Image of the Staff**: *The wizard leans on his staff as he calls forth his ally in the magic.*

**Three elven sisters: Amanda, Silver Flame, and Vanessa with staffs they just created at one of The Silver Elves magical parties.**

## Elven Spell Casting

**CHARGING SPELL:** (This spell is used to charge your wand, cane or staff with energy and power in order to fulfill your will.)
**"Power great this wand (or cane, etc.) does wield
To my will all willingly yield."**

(Arvyndase)
**"Eldro ralt wyr tald bålu yot
Va el'na yon wyl  yondasla ped."**

(Pronunciation)
Eel - drow rail-t were tale-d bah - lou yote
Vah eel'nah yone will yone - das - lah peed.

**PURPOSE SPELL:** (to dedicate your wand, cane or staff for a particular function or purpose)
**"This wand (or cane or staff) does bring success (or prosperity or love, etc.) my way
Its power increasing every day."**

(Arvyndase)
**"Wyr tald bålu cura reda el'na yer
Ter'na eldro memarndas lotym lea."**

Pronunciation)
Were tale-d bah - lou cur - rah re - dah eel'nah year
Tier'nah eel - drow me - mare'n - dace low - tim lee – ah.

**WAND SPELL:** (for increasing your will power and perseverance)
**"By the power of this wand I hold
The world about me, I now mold."**

(Arvyndase)
**"La tae eldro u wyr tald El gosp
Tae telth basar el, El mat mash."**

(Pronunciation)
Lah tay eel - drow you were tale-d Eel go-sp
Tay teal-th bay - sair eel, Eel mate may-sh.

**CANE SPELL:** (for increasing your powers of enchantment)
**"Powers increase as I do charm
And bring all good and never harm."**

(Arvyndase)
**"Eldroli memarn tat El ba elfat**
**Nar cura wyl ril nar konzar gras."**

(Pronunciation)
Eel - drow - lie me - mare-n tate Eel bah eel - fate
Nair cur - rah will rile nair cone - zair grace.

**STAFF SPELL:** (for increasing your knowledge and wizardly skills)
**"Knowledge, wisdom, wizard skill**
**The folk I serve be better still."**

(Arvyndase)
**"Kenvu, zardpos, zårdoa teld**
**Tae ehar El elser te rilfa vila."**

(Pronunciation)
"Keen - view, zair-d - poe-ss, zar - doe - ah teal-d
Tay e - hair Eel eel - sear tea rile - fah vie – lah."

"Elven Rangers are often instructed to 'Keep Their Ears Pointed' as they go scouting, which means be as silent as possible and listen carefully. On the other hand, young elves are frequently reminded to 'Keep their Ears Pointed Back', which means to listen carefully, even listen to rumors and gossip, but not believe everything that they hear."

"Elfin will touch you in ways that you hadn't realized were possible but had always hoped would be true."

"The Elves say that if the eyes are the windows of the soul, emotions are its walls and feelings its doors, and love and affection the keys to those doors, by which one may enter into the dwelling place of the spirit."

"The young magician asked the old elf, 'What do I do if I drop my wand in the middle of a ritual'. The wise old elf replied, 'You pick it up and go on with the ritual. Or you leave it lying there and go on with the ritual. Either way, you complete the ritual'."

# Chapter 24 . . . . Elven Witches' Spoons and Brooms

*lven witches need lots of spoons. Spoons are important in elven hedgewitchery for evoking magic and are closely associated with the cauldron or vessel for making magic happen. Besides using our spoons for stirring up the magic, we love to evoke healing by decorating our spoons with magical elven runes, elven sigils and spells and then displaying them on trays on the wall. This chapter will give you instructions on how to do this yourself. Before the magic may begin, however, the elven hedgewitch will need to do a little sweeping, purifying and cleansing. So we also have a section in this chapter on making magic brooms.

Seven magical elven witches' spoons set in a tray for display.
Later we decorated the tray with ivy and magical items and hung it above a doorway.

## Elven Witches' Spoons

**The Magical Image:** *The elven witch picks up her magical cooking spoon to cast a healing spell upon her brew.*

### Materials to Collect:
1. Sobo craft and fabric glue or other glue you like that works well
2. Wooden spoons (the light wood colored ones are best and use a variety of sizes, or whatever you can spare from your kitchen), you could also use plastic stirring spoons since you are going to paint over them anyway, but we prefer wood
3. A collection of beautiful specialty yarn (we love the yarn with glitter in it) and you only need a couple of feet of each. Also, there's yarn that is kind of fuzzy, that's very cool, too. Check out the yarn store. Ours came for free because a faerie-gnome sister housemate who was into knitting moved and left us some very lovely yarn.
4. A variety of beautiful buttons and old, sometimes broken jewelry
5. Acrylic paints and brushes (we suggest bright and deep colors) both light and dark. For the light you may wish to use white and silver. You will need both a fine tipped brush for painting the symbols and a larger brush for painting the entire spoon. Of course, you can use a paint pen, but they give off fumes and (as we have said) we try to avoid toxic fumes as much as possible.

### Directions:
First we painted seven plain wooden spoons (each were a different size and shape), in seven different colors (red, blue, yellow, green, orange, purple and white), representing to us the rays of the elven seven-pointed star. Of course, you may wish to begin with just a couple of spoons and let your imagination be your guide as to what colors you wish to use. Remember, it is your magic, your enchantment, trust your own feelings on this and other such matters.

After the painted spoons had dried, we used a fine tip brush and contrasting color to paint a variety of elven spirit sigils on the bowl part of the spoons (to find elven spirits you may wish to consult our book *The Elfin Book of Spirits: Evoking the Beneficent Powers of Faerie*). We encourage you to paint any symbol that you feel expresses your magic. We also used the seven-pointed star symbol as well. On one of the spoons we use a spirit sigil, but on another we used our elven runes (see *The Book of Elven Runes*), and still others we used our elven sigil system for writing out the spirits name in sigil form.

Next, we used a very fine brush to paint elven runes and also some magic healing spells in our elven language Arvyndase on some of the handles or on part of the handles. Once the spoons were completely dry, we glued beautiful buttons and jewels on the spoon handles, each having one or two. Next, we wrapped some of the handles in a variety of beautiful yarn, each different and coordinated with the color of the spoon. We did not cover any of the other decorations, of course. Once we made our seven magical spoons, we glued them on a woven wooden tray and took a picture of it for our Silver Elves cookery book cover (see *The Elf Folks Book of Cookery*).

Then, for the final step, we added some fabric ivy vines to the tray of spoons, weaving them around the outside and through the tray edge. To secure the ivy leaves, we glued them in places using Sobo Craft and Fabric Glue (we like the easy squeeze bottle that is made by Plaid Enterprises and sold at most local craft stores). You may need to glue a few leaves at a time. Also, we suggest that you invest in a clamp, as often when you are gluing fabric or paper, you will use this devise to hold the pieces together while the glue dries. We also glued a few other little objects—a seashell, an Hawaiian Tiki stirring stick for a drink, and a little red paper umbrella—on the edge of the tray to spice up the look of the display. This is where you can get quite creative and even place in the art some objects that have personal meaning and magic to you. Then to complete the process, we hung the magic tray up on the living room wall of our eald, over a doorway to the entrance of our elven treasures room.

Of course you may use the same process to make magic trays that house any magical objects or found natural objects that will fit in your tray and be light enough to hang on a wall. A magic tray is somewhat like a magic plate, although it is slightly different in that it is generally square or rectangle rather than a round shape and does not traditionally symbolize a pentacle. They can be used to hold an array of magical art pieces and/or found natural objects. It can be a type of reliquary in itself (see instructions for making reliquaries in a previous chapter). Often we use magical trays to hold and display on the wall in our Eald magical items that we have made. We even use them to cast a spell. Magical spells are easily written on small pieces of paper, rolled up, and hidden among the items glued on the tray if you desire part of your display and thus magic to be unseen.

## Elven Spell Casting

**COOKING SPELL:** (Use this spell to enchant your cooking and affect those who ingest it.)
**"Take in this magic, nurtured well**
**By the food instilled with this bright spell."**

(Arvyndase)
**"Rud ver wyr êldon, helïn darl**
**La tae lur waithïn ena wyr ilu moja."**

(Pronunciation)
Rude veer were l - doan, heal - in dare-l
Lah tay lure way - eye-th - in e - nah were eye - lou moe – jah.

**EMPOWERING SPELL, RED**: (for charging your spoon with first ray energy)
**"Strong and certain, confident
To guide and lead and not relent."**

(Arvyndase)
**"Mylth nar imsa, elim
Va foren nar ofor nar kon okor."**

(Pronunciation)
Mill-th nair I'm - sah, e - lime
Vah for - reen nair oh - for nair cone oh – core.

**EMPOWERING SPELL, BLUE**: (for charging your spoon with second ray energy)
**"Attracting love and loving are
True love comes by Elven star."**

(Arvyndase)
**"Chanadas kyêla nar kyêlådas da
Lod kyêla kosolu la Êldata mêl."**

(Pronunciation)
Chay - nay - dace key - l - lah nair key - l - lah - dace dah
Load key - l - lah co - so - lou lah L - day - tah mell.

**EMPOWERING SPELL, YELLOW**: (for charging your spoon with third ray energy)
**"Increasing wisdom, knowledge, too
Informs my life and all I do."**

(Arvyndase)
**"Memarndas zardpos, kenvu, bil
Leyanlu el'na ela nar wyl El ba."**

(Pronunciation)
Me - mare-n - dace zair-d - poe-ss, keen - view, bile
Lee - yane - lou eel'nah e - lah nair will Eel bah.

**EMPOWERING SPELL, WHITE, BLACK OR SILVER OR RAINBOW:** (for charging your spoon with fourth ray energy)
**"Wonders you do now create**
**Skill and inspiration mate."**

(Arvyndase)
**"Tyltålli le ba mat talys**
**Teld nar felidur erni."**

(Pronunciation)
Till - tahl lee bah mate tay - liss
Teal-d nair fee - lie - dure ear – nigh.

**EMPOWERING SPELL, GREEN:** (for charging your spoon with fifth ray energy)
**"Every skill that I desire**
**My abilities growing ever higher."**

(Arvyndase)
**"Lotym teld dij El nalo**
**El'na ashatuli lythdas vari altfa."**

(Pronunciation)
Low - tim teal-d dye-j Eel nay - low
Eel'nah a - shay - two - lie lith - dace vay - rye ale-t – fah.

**EMPOWERING SPELL, ORANGE:** (for charging your spoon with sixth ray energy)
**"Devoted to your vision true**
**Dedication informs all you do."**

(Arvyndase)
**"Tolåïn va le'na jilo lod**
**Teyådur leyanlu wyl le ba."**

(Pronunciation)
Toe - lah - in vah lee'nah jie - low load
Tea - yah - dure lee - yane - lou will lee bah.

**EMPOWERING SPELL, PURPLE:** (for charging your spoon with seventh ray energy)
**"Deep the secrets you do find**
**About yours'elf and elfin kind."**

(Arvyndase)
**"Dorae tae marynli le ba làc**
**Basar le'eln nar êldat faed."**

(Pronunciation)
Door - ray tay may - ren - lie lee bah lock
Bay - sair lee'eel-n nair l -date fae – eed.

**(Note our color attributions are different than some might have them, who would have fourth as green, fifth are orange, sixth as violet and seventh as indigo. Feel free to use the associations that feel right to you.)**

## Witches Brooms

The witches broom is a traditional symbol of a witch's power to fly, which is to say rise to the higher planes of consciousness and realization. In creating a witch's broom, you are evoking greater realization, understanding and connection to, and ability at evoking the eldritch powers, the supernatural world, and the preternatural realms. The witch's broom is sometimes called a besom and beside flying it symbolizes and is actually used for purification: sweeping and cleaning, and in some pagan traditions a couple gets married by jumping over the broom, thus it has a uniting, sealing and bonding symbolism.

**The Magical Image:** *A witch's broom rests in the corner of her hut.*

## Materials to Collect:

- A broom, an old one, a new one, a wooden one with straw, or plastic, or metal with plastic 'twigs' or whatever you can find, or:
- You can make your own, using trigs, straw, palm branch leaves that have fallen from a palm tree. Corn husks, or, in our case, from molted wing feathers from a peacock.
- You will need a handle, so a sturdy stick long enough for a broom handle, or in our case, a cane that we decorated;
- Paint, brushes, or engraving tool.
- Sealant.
- Possibly twine, string, ribbon or wire if you are making your own from scratch
- Decorative elements, such as ribbon, buttons or anything you'd like to attach to or hang from your broom.

## Directions:

If you are using an already constructed broom, you just need to add whatever runes, sigils, or symbols you wish to charge it with you magic and any talismans that appeal to you.

If you are making your own, you need a basic pole of some sort, and either a bunch of twigs, straw or other dried long weeds, palm fronds bundled together and attached by twine or wire to the pole, or as in our case, feathers bundled together and attached to a cane (see photo on the right of Silver Flame sweeping with our elven witches broom we made with a cane as the handle and bundled molted peafowl wing feathers as the broom head). And then decorate the pole or cane with the symbols of your magic. If you engrave symbols you can put paint inside of them, or if you just use paint you may also wish to use sealant to help them endure.

Note that there is an old tradition called bundling in which couples who were engaged would sleep together fully clothed to get to know each other better. This seems to reinforce the idea of jumping over the broom as a symbol of commitment to each other.

## Elven Spell Casting

**FLYING SPELL:** (Use this spell for increasing your skill, knowledge and abilities in magic and evolving to greater heights of understanding and power.)
**"To the heights I will ascend
Increasing powers do portend."**

(Arvyndase)
**"Va tae altarli El yon rystar
Memarndas eldroli ba imfad."**

(Pronunciation)
Vah tay ale - tayr - lie Eel yone riss - tayr
Me - mare-n - dace eel - drow - lie bah I'm – fade.

**PURIFICATION SPELL:** (for sweeping away the old and clearing the way for the new)
**"The past is swept away at last**
**The future looms and it is vast**
**The present opens now the way**
**To greater things this very day."**

(Arvyndase)
**"Tae log da komïn faron zan zas**
**Tae lasel almolu nar ter da sud**
**Tae hårna carolu mat tae yer**
**Va raltfa vessåli wyr lefa lea."**

(Pronunciation)
Tay low-g dah comb - in fay - rone zane zay-ss
Tay lay - seal ale - moe - lou nair tier dah sued
Tay har - nah car - row - lou mate tay year
Vah rail-t - fah vee-s - sah - lie were lee - fah lee – ah.

**DEVOTION SPELL:** (for increasing the power of union between individuals)
**"By this broom we are united**
**All our visions are requited."**

(Arvyndase)
**"La wyr wash eli da atåraïn**
**Wyl eli'na jiloli da abakïn."**

(Pronunciation)
Lah were waysh e - lie dah a - tah - ray - in
Will e - lie'nah jie - low - lie dah a - bake – in.

**"The elves believe the Soul is a sensory organ for connecting with others."**

**"Love is as true as the things that we do."**
**—Olde Elven Saying**

# Chapter 25 . . . . Wishing Wheels

When our two children were very young, we went to a Covenant of the Goddess gathering at a local hot springs resort where hundreds of witches and magic wielders had gathered. Among, them was a young witch whose father was an old time traditional ceremonial magician. Later, in the year, we decided to attend a Spiral Dance ceremony being held in San Francisco that would be lead by Starhawk. Since our new witch friend and her father lived just over the bridge from San Francisco, they invited us to stay overnight at their house before going to the Spiral Dance, thus making things a lot more convenient in terms of time and travel for us.

As it happened, the witch's father had the equivalent of an esoteric bookstore and occult museum in one of the rooms of their house and he kindly gave us a guided tour. Among the items there was a Prayer Wheel of the Buddhist sort that our son took an immediate liking to. The other thing that he liked in their home, however, and liked a good deal more, was a small dog and, of course, he immediately wished he had a dog of his own. As it was, when he was home he would get up very early in the morning, way too early, and gather up all the loose dogs nearby in our neighborhood and take them for walks along the creek and up the side of the mountain that was behind our eald. He told us once when he was quite young, "Dog makes life good!" and we quite agree.

So, when we got home from the Spiral Dance event, we decided to make our son and our daughter Wishing Wheels, our elven version of the Buddhist Prayer Wheel. We promised our son that someday, when we came across one and could afford it, we'd get him a genuine one (that promise only took about 30 years to fulfill, we always keep our promises although it can take us a while to do so) but in the meantime, we got together what we needed and made him a Wishing Wheel so he could spin it (he loved spinning things and would often spin a pencil in his hand as he thought and pondered things). So we had him put inside the wishing wheel a wish on a piece of paper for the dog that he so desired. Every time, he looked a bit forlorn about getting a dog, we would tell him to spin that wheel. And in fact, very shortly thereafter, one of the local dogs we had not seen previously began showing up frequently at our back door. Soon after, the dog wound up in the pound and his owners didn't want to bother to retrieve him, so we did and he became our dog.

**The Magical Image:** *The elf child spins a wishing wheel to fulfill his desires.*

**Our first homemade prayer wheel made from a condensed milk can, made in 1987, now over 30 years old and still working its magic.**

## Materials to Collect:

- A tin can about the size of a soup can or condensed milk can.
- The screw on lid to a jar that would fit perfectly inside the can.
- A dowel rod.
- A screw.
- A chain and two nuts and bolts.
- Images (from magazines or printed from the internet) to paste to the outside of the wishing wheel.
- Tape.
- Or, paints, bushes, etc.

## Directions:

Eat your soup or whatever is contained in the can. It is best if you have one of those Japanese can openers that don't leave a sharp edge after opening, but we don't think they had been invented yet when we made ours so we just used a pair of pliers to bend in the sharp edges, after thoroughly washing the can and letting it dry.

We found a screw top for a jar that fit perfectly into the can.

We drilled a small hole in what would be the top of the wishing wheel (originally the bottom of the can) so a screw would go through it without sticking (it has to spin easily). So the types of screws that have a short smooth space beneath the head and the screw spiral is best.

We drilled another, slightly bigger hole through the screw on the jar top, so the dowel rod would fit through it easily but fairly closely.

We pasted the images we had collected around the side and on the top, but you could paint yours and add magical symbols or whatever evoked your wishes.

We made another hole in the topside of the can. We had a screw bolt with a nut and we put it through the small chain and secured it with a bolt on the other side of the chain, to give it weight and help the wheel to spin around (this is really important), and we attached another screw bolt to the other end of the chain and then put the bolt through the hole in the upper side of the can and secured it inside with its nut.

Then we put the screw through the top of the can and screwed it into the top of the dowel rod in such a way to allow the can to spin easily around the screw and rod.

Then we slipped the screw top of the jar onto the dowel rod and pushed it up until the lid fit into the open bottom (previously top) of the can.

The photo on the right is of Silver Flame and Zardoa in 1987 testing out the newly made prayer wheel.

Here's the rub though. If your jar top doesn't fit snuggly into the can, you may need to tape it or glue it closed. We taped ours, even though that wasn't very elegant, because we thought that our elflings might want to replace the wishes they'd put inside from time to time. But if you don't plan to change your wish you can glue yours closed, which certainly looks less messy or rinky-dink, but remember what's important for hedgewitchery is mainly the power of the intention, not the elegance of our creation. We're going for effectivity over style in this case, but if you can achieve style, too, that is a decided bonus and even better.

And that's it. Now you can spin your wishes into the Universe.

## Elven Spell Casting

**EMPOWERING SPELL:** (Use to charge and power up your Elven Wishing Wheel.)
**"Every wish will come to be**
**As each spin does set it free**
**Going forth the stars aspire**
**Returning hence with our desire."**

(Arvyndase)

"Lotym felj yon koso va te

Tat cha solo bålu pånd ter alo

Tasdas soch tae mêlli watan

Cunbadas nynse ena eli'na nalo."


(Pronunciation)

Low - tim feel-j yone co - so vah tea

Tate chah so - low bah - lou pond tier a - low

Tace - dace so-ch tay mell - lie way - tane

Cun - bay - dace nin - see e - nah e - lie'nah nay – low.


WISH SPELL: (for fulfilling a particular desire or wish)

"Wishing, wishing fervently

All I wish will come to me

Success (or health or a dog) is mine for all to see

Arriving now quite readily."


(Arvyndase)

"Feljdas, feljdas alfevla

Wyl El felj yon koso va el

Reda da el'na fro wyl va ten

Komaldas mat ven anitla."


(Pronunciation)

Feel-j - dace, feel-j - dace ale - feev - lah

Will Eel feel-j yone co - so vah eel

Re - dah dah eel'nah fro will vah teen

Co - male - dace mate veen a - night – lah.

"The Elves say: Our lives are like ships at sea. We may not have control over the waves, tides and other circumstances we face, but we need to have mastery over the ship we are sailing."

"Elfin doesn't just await us, it also reaches out to us, sounding Its Call, which echoes in the hearts and minds of all true Elfae folk."

"If you don't get up in the morning, get up in the afternoon." Olde Elven Saying meaning if you don't realize your dreams right away, don't give up on them.

# Chapter 26 . . . . Pan Pipes and Other Magical Woodwork

## Pan Pipes

First, we should say that these elves have a long time association with the Great God Pan, the satyr of Greek Myth. And while we don't worship him as a god, we do honor him greatly and feel very close to him. He is an ancient friend and associate or accomplice, you might say, of these elves.

Ages ago we had a scrap of light blue print cloth that was energized in a Elven Tantric Ritual involving our love of Pan and each other and later we cut this cloth into strips and left the pieces in places we felt had a strong resonance with this Pan energy, including Forever Forests and other places in California. We still have a piece of it that is wrapped around the ankle of a teraphim in our home, a sweet, young faun named Feather, who we have shown you in a photo in an earlier chapter.

We also came upon some panpipes at a used goods store one day and decided, since we had bamboo growing near us, to attempt to make our own panpipes using the one we had acquired as a model. While the tone isn't perfect, it was pretty good for our first attempt.

Left: Pan Pipes we made; Right: Pan Pipes we bought and used as a model.

**The Magical Image:** *The enchantress brings forth the magic of faerie with songs.*

## Materials to collect:

- You need bamboo, however, since you are seeking to have different tones, you can use one length of bamboo that you cut at different places along its length. Cut it so that you cut just beneath the joint, which is usually solid and closed off, and then further up where the bamboo shaft is open. You will need to cut different lengths for slightly different tones.

- Glue and string.

## Directions:

Find and cut your bamboo pieces at slightly varied lengths, getting longer as you go along (or shorter if that is your preference). Blow down the open end and see how it sounds. Testing is important. It's the same as blowing down an old fashion glass pop or soda bottle. If you like the sound, cut the open end of the bamboo at a slight angle from the middle of the top, instead of cutting totally across, so that half the top still preserves the flat angle.

Cut one piece right down the middle, the two sides will be used to go across the various sized pieces and hold them together. One you will put straight across all the pieces, the other will go at an angle parallel to the angle of your different sized pieces (as in the photo on the left on the previous page). You can tie the various pieces together (we had eight pieces), interweaving them with the two sidepieces. You might find that hot glue or another glue will help secure it as well.

You may wish to cut a bunch of different lengths and test their sounds and then put the ones that work best together.

## Elven Spell Casting

"On His Throne sits Pan, He wakes the Magic Again. He wakes the Magic Again, Again! He wakes the Magic Again." (We often sing and dance this spell while we do our art and while we use it in magic intention.)

**BARDIC SPELL:** (Use this spell to give your pan pipes bardic powers.)
**"As my tunes go forth, are heard**
**Listeners harken to my word."**

(Arvyndase)
**"Tat el'na nisli tas soch, da lysïn**
**Farsofåli artta va el mol."**

(Pronunciation)
Tate eel'nah nice - lie tace sow-ch, dah liss - in
Fair - so - fah - lie air-t - tah vah eel mole.

**ENCHANTING SPELL:** (Use this spell so that those who hear your pipes will be enchanted and inspired, especially romantically.)
**"The sounds of love do touch your heart
And awaken romance from the start."**

(Arvyndase)
**"Tae dethli u kyêla ba fost le'na bom
Nar vasåta faerla an tae altu."**

(Pronunciation)
Tay dee-th - lie key - l - lah bah foe-st lee'nah bow-m
Nair vay - -sah - tah fay - ear - lah ane tay ale –two.

## Wooden Door Piece

We found a nice board one time and decided to wood-burn on it and create an elven piece for the entrance to our eald. We drew vines with leaves about the outer edges and put Arvyndase script in the center (see a photo of this magical board on the next page). Originally, we thought about creating one for the other side of the door and then for the lintel piece but we never quite got around to that, at least not as yet. Still, we loved this piece and had it in out eald for decades and eventually, when we moved to Hawaii, our daughter asked if she could have it, so we passed it on to her.

## Materials to collect:

- A piece of wood of whatever size. We used one that was about six feet tall, six or so inches wide, and about an inch thick.
- Wood burning tool, or magnifying glass.
- Your design for the piece.
- Sealant
- Maybe glitter.

## Directions:

We drew our design on to the wood, and then we started with our wood burner, but soon found that for us it was easier and more fun to just sit in the sunlight with a magnifying glass and burn it in that way.

After we were done, and actually wrote what the Arvyndase said on the front of it in English, we also wrote on the back lower corner, "Made by Elves" there in small print, our artist's signature. Then we painted clear sealant over the entire piece. This took several coats.

Then, just as the last coat of the sealant was nearly dry but still sticky we blew very fine silver glitter over the piece, to gave it that bit of extra elven magic.

## Elven Spell Casting

If you are doing this for your eald, or elven home, you might wish to put the name of your elf home upon it. Have you named your eald? Ours is named Eldafaryn or Elf Haven.

EALD SPELL: (for blessing your elven home)
**"Blessings on this elven space**
**Be it ever filled with grace."**

(Arvyndase)
**"Elsordasli ton wyr êldata noth**
**Te ter vari ulåïn ena felsh."**

(Pronunciation)
Eel - soar - dace - lie tone were l - day - tah no-th
Tea tier vay - rye you - lah - in e - nah feel-sh

ENERGIZING SPELL: (Use this spell for empowering whatever place you put your elven sign or for whatever you wish to energize.)
**"Power burnt into this wood**
**Magic comes with all that's good."**

(Arvyndase)
**"Eldro lazïn verva wyr ålti**
**Êldon kosolu ena wyl dij'da ril."**

(Pronunciation)
Eel - drow layz - in veer - vah were all - tie
L - doan co - so - lou e - nah will dye-j'dah rile.

# Chapter 27 . . . . Magic Tables

Wͤe treat our magic tables, tables full of magic, or altars as most people call them, as works of art and they are full of enchantment and life. This is the place that we like to merge our magic with our art, for it is on a table as the one in the photo above that we do all our meditations for elven blessings. You can see that this is a "magic worktable" really, where we burn our candles, read our spells and cast our elven enchantments. Here we are going for effectivity of our magic work rather than aesthetics of

the table appearance. You can, as we did in the above photo, just find a table and put your magic on it, creating an aura of magic and enchantment in the flow of the symbolic objects and magical tools as they rest upon it. In our case, we happened to come upon a large copper table top with a five pointed star on it at a garage sale for a mere $20. It was probably from the Middle East or India originally. It was quite a deal and a blessing of magical elven luck, surely. Here on the left is the same copper table as in the first photo, now set up for a special Rainbow Dragon Full Moon Magic Circle. When sharing the magic in a group circle, we do consider the aesthetics of the table arrangement to also be an important aspect of the enchantment magic. If you look around our eald, you will find both rather wild looking 'magic worktables' where we do our daily magics and also magic tables where the magic is set up with beauty and symmetry as well.

We have also taken old tables and painted symbols and designs upon them. In one case, we found a low rectangular wooden coffee table and painted the Elven Tree of Life upon it (see our book *The Elven Tree of Life Eternal*), which we used to help people understand the situations and circumstances of their life by referring to the various sephiroth on the tree and their interactions. But we could easily have used it as a magic table as well.

**The Magical Image:** *The magician creates Hir magic table as a work of art and brings forth healing magick for her faerie kin.*

## Materials to collect:

- A table.
- Your magical tools and the symbols of your magic.
- Paint, if you are decorating the surface yours'elf. And, of course, brushes.
- A colored pencil that will show up on your table top, for drawing if you are decorating it with symbols you will be painting.
- Sealant. Always seal your paint and your magic if you wish it to last. A lesson we learned over time.

## Directions:

If you are using your magic table as an art presentation, than it is just about making your magical table and the contents on it as enchanting, alluring and pleasing as possible.

If you are creating your own table (not just setting it with magical items shown on the previous page), you need the basic design of what you will paint on it, or if you wish engrave, or wood-burn. Draw your design on first to see how it looks and use it as your guide as you paint or carve or whatever. It will be so much easier that way. And afterwards give it a few coats of sealant to protect and preserve it, chanting your spells as it dries.

## Elven Spell Casting

ENCHANTING SPELL: (Use to energize and empower your magic table.)
**"Ever charging power grows**
**Enchantment wondrous ever shows**
**Increasing secrets I do know**
**Into my magic it does flow."**

(Arvyndase)
**"Vari fylredas eldro lythlu
Syrandir tyltålsey vari tekelu
Memarndas marynli El ba ken
Verva el'na êldon ter bålu shur."**

(Pronunciation)
Vay - rye fill - re - dace eel - drow lith - lou
Sir - rain - dire till - tahl - say vay - rye tea - key - lou
Me - mare-n - dace may - ren - lie Eel bah keen
Veer - vah eel'nah l - doan tier bah - lou sure.

"When the stars shine upon the elves, the elves shine back."
—What the Eldar Say

"The logic of the elves includes their feelings and intuition. For some facts can be seen clearly but others are hidden and must be sensed from what is already known."

"Elves catch dreams to weave anew, magic futures that are true
Elfin on the Earth is born, upon this bright and shining morn."

"If the world you live in isn't elfin, transform it. That's what elven magic is all about."
—Old Elven Saying

"When you first realize you're an elf, Elfin begins to appear all around you. It is not really the world that has changed but your perception of it."

"Faerie shines its radiance on all, but not all are ready to perceive its glow."
—Ancient Elven Knowledge

"The New Dawn of Elfin is first perceived in the hearts of those who love it."

# Chapter 28 . . . . The Orb of Healing

**Our faerie sister, Michiko Spring, holds the Orb of Healing,
enchanting it with her love and healing magic, and
receiving healing in return from this most magical orb.**

The Orb of Healing is perhaps our most empowered magical artifact. We say this because we have had it for over four decades and it has been in every Magic Elven Circle that we have ever shared with our elven tribe, and each time it has accumulated more and more magic. We created the mantra "Healing is Contagious; Pass it Around" that we chant whenever we pass it among ours'elves in our Magical Elven Circles.

The Orb of Healing is truly the center of our magic. When it is not being used in an Elven Magical Circle, it is always resting in the center of one of our magic tables. Presently, it radiates from the center of a magic table in our bedroom. And every night when we turn out the lights and go to bed, the Orb of Healing gives forth its greenish glow and sends its healing rays all over the room. We fall to sleep with its light enchanting us and giving us gentle dreams of Elfin.

**The Magical Image:** *Each elf blesses the Orb of Healing and then hands it to the next elf in the magic circle saying: "Healing is Contagious, Pass it Around!"*

## Materials to Collect:

- An orb, crystal ball, or in our case: a glass float that was used in the past by fishermen in Asia to keep their fishing nets from sinking, as well as their longlines or droplines afloat.
- Florescent glow-in the-dark paint (we use green).

## Directions:

Paint your orb with several coats of florescent paint, letting each coat dry separately. We usually give our orb a new coat of paint about every ten years. Other than that, there is not much else to do art wise, for the real effort is in the magic and use of the orb.

You will surely wish to do as we have and as we continue to do, to instill healing energy daily into the orb. And also you may use it when you are beginning to feel a bit sick or that your immune system is lower. You can use the orb absorbing its healing energy whenever you need it. You may also use it on your magic table to put healing energy into other magical items and out into your eald.

You may also wish to keep in mind and fashion your spell in charging your orb with the understanding that it may break one day. We realize that because the Orb of Healing is made of glass, one day either when it is with us or has moved into other hands, it will be broken. But its magic is such that when this happens, all the healing energy that has accumulated through the years will be released and radiate healing around the Earth and back and then unto the Stars, with a signal of healing to all our elfae kindred, wherever they may be.

## Elven Spell Casting

**"Healing is Contagious;**
**Pass It Around!"**

In Arvyndase:
**"Hyrndas da Desåsey**
**Gol Ter Anabo!"**

Herne – dace dah Dee – sah – say;
Goal Tear A – nay – bow!

# Final Word!

This is a book of Elven Hedgewitchery and as you have seen, it isn't really about doing things exactly the way we have done them but about inspiring you, as much as possible, to look around your own elven home and the environment you live in and see what is easily, freely or inexpensively available to you so you may create your own elven art, magic pieces, clothes and other items to manifest Elfin in your own life and for your kindred, and in that way express your individual elfae nature.

Also, collect, collect, collect, especially those things that others have failed to see the value in but are still wonders to your eyes. We promise you, if you do this and use your magical collections to create enchanted art and elven fashion, more treasures will come to you, out of the blue and from the Mists of Faerie and the Twilight Realms of Elfin.

"Elf witches are much like other witches, except instead of attempting to make particular things happen as we desire, we seek to assist Nature to fulfill Destiny perfectly. For that is what we truly desire, anyway." —The Silver Elves

# About the Authors

The Silver Elves, Zardoa and Silver Flame, are a family of elves who have been living and sharing the Elven Way since 1975. They are the authors of 45+ books on magic and enchantment and the Elven Way, available on Amazon internationally, and your local bookstore, including:

*The Book of Elven Runes: A Passage Into Faerie;*

*The Magical Elven Love Letters, volumes I, 2, and 3;*

*An Elfin Book of Spirits: Evoking the Beneficent Powers of Faerie;*

*Caressed by an Elfin Breeze: The Poems of Zardoa Silverstar;*

*Eldafaryn: True Tales of Magic from the Lives of the Silver Elves;*

*Arvyndase (Silverspeech): A Short Course in the Magical Language of the Silver Elves;*

*The Elven Book of Dreams: A Magical Oracle of Faerie;*

*The Book of Elven Magick: The Philosophy and Enchantments of the Seelie Elves, Volume 1 & 2;*

*What An Elf Would Do: A Magical Guide to the Manners and Etiquette of the Faerie Folk;*

*The Elven Tree of Life Eternal: A Magical Quest for One's True S'Elf;*

*Magic Talks: On Being a Correspondence Between the Silver Elves and the Elf Queen's Daughters;*

*Sorcerers' Dialogues: A Further Correspondence Between the Silver Elves and the Founders of the Elf Queen's Daughters;*

*Discourses on High Sorcery: More Correspondence Between the Silver Elves and the Founders of the Elf Queen's Daughters;*

*Ruminations on Necromancy: Continuing Correspondence Between the Silver Elves and the Founders of the Elf Queen's Daughter;*

*The Elven Way: The Magical Path of the Shining Ones;*

*Through the Mists of Faerie: A Magical Guide to the Wisdome Teachings of the Ancient Elven;*

*The Book of Elf Names: 5,600 Elven Names to Use for Magic, Game Playing, Inspiration, Naming One's Self and One's Child, and as Words in the Elven Language of the Silver Elves;*

*Elven Silver: The Irreverent Faery Tales of Zardoa Silverstar;*

*An Elven Book of Ryhmes: Book Two of the Magical Poems of Zardoa Silverstar;*

*The Voice of Faerie: Making Any Tarot Deck Into an Elven Oracle;*

*Liber Aelph: Words of Guidance from the Silver Elves to our Magical Children;*

*The Shining Ones: The Elfin Spirits That Guide You According to Your Birth Date and the Evolutionary Lessons They Offer;*

*Living the Personal Myth: Making the Magic of Faerie Real in One's Own Personal Life;*

*Elf Magic Mail, The Original Letters of the Elf Queen's Daughters with Comentary by the Silver Elves, Book 1 and 2;*

*The Elves of Lyndarys: A Magical Tale of Modern Faerie Folk;*

*The Elf Folk's Book of Cookery: Recipes For a Delighted Tongue, a Healthy Body and a Magical Life;*

*Faerie Unfolding: The Cosmic Expression of the Divine Magic;*

*The Elements of Elven Magic: A New View of Calling the Elementals Based Upon the Periodic Table of Elements;*

*The Keys to Elfin Enchantment: Mastery of the Faerie Light Through the Portals of Manifestation;*

*Elf Quotes: A Collection of Over 1000 Ancient Elven Sayings and Wise Elfin Koans by The Silver Elves About Magic and The Elven Way;*

*The United States of Elfin Imagining A More Elven Style of Government;*

*Elven Geomancy: An Ancient Oracle of the Elfin Peoples for Divination and Spell Casting;*

*Creating Miracles In the Modern World: The Way Of the Elfin Thaumaturge;*

*The Magical Realms of Elfin: Answers to Questions About Being an Elf and Following the Elven Path, Volume 1;*

*Manifesting Elfin: Answers to Questions About Being an Elf and Following the Elven Path, Volume 2;*

*Elven Psychology: Understanding the Elfin Psyche and the Evolutionary and Esoteric Purpose of Mental Disorders;*

*The Elves Say: A Collection of Over 1000 Ancient Elven Sayings and Wise Elfin Koans by The Silver Elves About Magic and The Elven Way, Volume 2;*

*The Complete Dictionary of Arvyndase: The Elven Language of The Silver Elves;* and

*Sticks and Stones, Feathers, Charms and Bones: An Original Oracle of the Elfin Peoples of the Ancient Future.*

*Elf Tribes: The Silver Elves' Guide for Finding Your Magical Kind and Kin;* and it's companion book

*Faerie, Fae and Otherkin: The Silver Elves' Guide for Finding Your Magical Kind and Kin.*

The Silver Elves have had various articles published in Circle Network News Magazine since 1986 and have given out over 6,000 elven names to interested individuals in the Arvyndase language, with each elf name having a unique meaning specifically for that person. They are also interviewed and mentioned numerous times in *Not In Kansas Anymore* by Christine Wicker (Harper San Francisco, 2005) and in *A Field Guide to Otherkin* by Lupa (Megalithica Books, 2007), and are discussed in Nikolay Lyapanenko's recent book *The Elves From Ancient Times To Our Days: The Magical Heritage of "Starry People" and their Continuation Into the Modern World* (2017) that gives a detailed account of their involvement in the Elven

Movement since 1975. Also, an interview with The Silver Elves is included in Emily Carding's recent popular book *Faery Craft* (Llewellyn Publications, 2012*)*. The Silver Elves understand the world as a magical or miraculous phenomena, and that all beings, by pursuing their own true path, will become whomever they truly desire to be.

You are welcome to explore The Silver Elves' website at **http://silverelves.angelfire.com**, visit their blog site at **https://thesilverelves.blogspot.com** on the Elven Way and also their blog site on Elven Lifestyle, Magic and Enchantment at **https://silverelves.wordpress.com**, and join them on Facebook with the names as "Michael J. Love (Zardoa of The SilverElves)" and "Martha Char Love (SilverFlame of The SilverElves)."

**The Silver Elves also invite you to come join them in some of their elven and magical otherkin Facebook groups where you will find the elven-faerie-fae otherkin community interacting and sharing the Elven Way:**

**The Magical Books of the Silver Elves —**
https://www.facebook.com/groups/539205916250397_— And if you would like to find out more about our Silver Elves books on The Elven Way, please do join us! We have discussions about our Silver Elves books as well as about Elven and Otherkin philosophy, elven lifestyle and the Elven Way and everything Elfin. If you have read our books and would like to discuss them with us, this is the place to come join in the discussions and share with us your reesponses.

**Elf Witches of the Mystic Moon —**
https://www.facebook.com/groups/806583242768352

**The Elven Way and Friends —**
https://www.facebook.com/groups/165938637423212 —A group for all our elven kin and friends to gather and share in discussions about The Elven Way and elvish life.

**Elven Life and Magic**
https://www.facebook.com/groups/629491797123886

**Elvish Magical Chat —**
https://www.facebook.com/groups/307775362744491

**The Faerie Circle —**
https://www.facebook.com/groups/1025483294180077

**Faerie Craft —**
https://www.facebook.com/groups/395403367195312 — This is a group to share and advertise your elven and fae artistic creations.

**I Heart Elven Magic —**
https://www.facebook.com/groups/2215672296

**United Otherkin Alliance —**
https://www.facebook.com/groups/328253710566869 This is an alliance for Otherkin/ Therians, where elves, faeries, dragons, kitsune, gnomes, hobbits, merkin, pixies, brownies, nymphs, driads, niaids, valkyrie, vampires, devas, fauns, unicorns, animal kin and all manner of Faerie Folk gather and come together! This group is open to anyone who wishes to be part of a congenial group of Otherkin.

**Feasting With the Elves** (come join us, we are just having some fun sharing elven recipes and healthy eating) — https://www.facebook.com/groups/597948240617006

**Devayana: Buddhism, Vedic, & Asian Spirituality for Elves and Fae**
https://www.facebook.com/groups/devayana
Nature & the Unseen Realms with the Elves & otherkin. A spiritual journey — https://www.facebook.com/groups/196916350335537

**Have you always wanted to hear elves speak in Arvyndase, the magical language of The Silver Elves?** Come listen! The Silver Elves just published their first You Tube video in their new The Silver Elves channel. And they would love it if you would please subscribe, like and comment! **https://youtu.be/unUkxT9QbNE**

"You can search for Elfin for what seems like forever and never find it.
You can wait for it to come and it never seems to arrive.
But if you live the life Elfin,
It emerges all around you
Like buds in the springtime."
—The Silver Elves

"Some folks speak of midnight as the Witching Hour.
We elves speak of the Enchanting Time,
Which is when our beloved kindred arrive."
—The Silver Elves

Printed in Poland
by Amazon Fulfillment
Poland Sp. z o.o., Wrocław

54121282R00123